NBC & ME:
MY LIFE AS A PAGE IN A BOOK

A MOCK MEMOIR OF MY BIG '80s DAZE WITH THE PEACOCK NETWORK

by Herbie J Pilato

Foreword by
Gretchen Harris Keskeys

Dedicated to the art of self-depreciation.

"The world is a book, and those who do not travel read only a page."

— St Augustine of Hippo

NBC & ME: My Life As A Page In a Book
© 2008 Herbie J Pilato. All Rights Reserved.
No part of this book may be reproduced in any form or by any means, electronic, mechanical, digital, photocopying or recording, except for the inclusion in a review, without permission in writing from the publisher.

Published in the USA by:
BearManor Media
P O Box 71426
Albany, Georgia 31708
WWW.BEARMANORMEDIA.COM

ISBN 1-59393-131-X

Printed in the United States of America.
Cover design and photo selection, editing, and layout by Matt Hankinson.
Text editing by Jaclyn Garfinkel.
Book design by Brian Pearce.

Table Of Contents

Foreword by Gretchen Harris Keskeys 9

Introduction 11

CHAPTER 1: Gimme A Break 17

CHAPTER 2: The Ties That Found Me 19

CHAPTER 3: The NBC Parking Lot 23

CHAPTER 4: Return to Mayberry 25

CHAPTER 5: The Star Treks Commence 29

CHAPTER 6: Miami's Nice & Vice 31

CHAPTER 7: The Night I Rode With Rider 33

CHAPTER 8: Fox Back In The Fold 35

CHAPTER 9: AirCourt '84 39

CHAPTER 10: The Golden Girls 41

CHAPTER 11: The Big Events 45

CHAPTER 12: **I Dreamt Of Jeannie** 45

CHAPTER 13: **I Remember Mama** 47

CHAPTER 14: **Krystle Blue Persuasion** 49

CHAPTER 15: **Pain Jane** 51

CHAPTER 16: **Donahue!** 55

CHAPTER 17: **Law & Order** 57

CHAPTER 18: **I Dreamt Of Jeannie: 15 Years Later** 59

CHAPTER 19: **Page On A Wire** 61

CHAPTER 20: **The Screaming Room** 61

Photos of Pages on Several Pages 66

CHAPTER 21: **A Page In The L.A. Times** 93

CHAPTER 22: **Super Passwords** 95

CHAPTER 23: **Is It Door Number 1 or Door Number 2?** 99

CHAPTER 24: **My Own Personal Carmen Miranda** 101

CHAPTER 25: **The Australian British Aisles** 105

CHAPTER 26: **The Ticket Orifice** 107

CHAPTER 27: **Exhausted!** 109

CHAPTER 28: **Hangin' With Rear Lobby Joe** 111

CHAPTER 29: **Vanna Speaks (with Brian Wilson)** 115

CHAPTER 30: **Harvey Levin Is Not Brandon Tartikoff** 119

CHAPTER 31: **I Helped Make A Wish Come True** 121

CHAPTER 32:	**Tabitha, Marilyn and Susie Lynn**	125
CHAPTER 33:	**My Endless Dateline with NBC**	129
CHAPTER 34:	**The Victory Page Tour**	131
CHAPTER 35:	**Dimples**	135
CHAPTER 36:	**Cheers**	139
CHAPTER 37:	**Mr. Excitement**	141
CHAPTER 38:	**My Photo Session With Brooke Shields**	145
CHAPTER 39:	**A Rivers Runs Through It**	149
CHAPTER 40:	**Shadow Dancing**	151
CHAPTER 41:	**I Stumped The Band (And Just About Everybody Else)**	153

Afterword 156

About the Author 159

Foreword by Gretchen Harris Keskeys

I have always viewed my time at NBC as a Page as a privilege. It was a dream job for a girl who longed to know what "really went on behind the scenes" of my favorite TV shows. Watching *The Tonight Show* growing up, I would often fantasize about what happened after the show. Surely, they all continued the party and everyone was friends!

But no — it didn't always turn out that way. I learned that the people you see on television aren't always like the characters we love. Some, like Michael Landon are as kind and genuine in real life as the dad he played on *Little House on the Prairie*. The others? Well, we'll leave the others alone. Better yet, I'll leave that up to Herbie J!

Now, Herbie J — he is the real deal. I had lost touch with him after our Page days ended (back in 1985). Then, following the death of Johnny Carson (in 2005), which brought back many wonderful *Tonight Show* clips, I did some serious reminiscing of those days. And one of the first people who came to my mind was Herbie J.

When I arrived at NBC, I was so nervous and intimidated and a very sensitive young woman. I wanted desperately to be liked and I could hardly take an unfriendly face. Meeting Herbie J was like running into an old friend at the most needed time. He was the quintessential Page: funny, entertaining, enthusiastic, full of dreams and truly a nice guy with a great smile. A real *for you* person. Those are the people you always remember and for whom you are forever grateful. Herbie is one of those people.

I am so pleased we reconnected and I think he is the one Page to write this book. Herbie remembers details about life at NBC that I had long forgotten. But, once I read his story, everything came back in *living color*!

Thank you, Herbie J, for taking us all on one of your "can't miss" tours of the Peacock Network.

Introduction

From May 1984 to December 1985, I worked as a Guest Relations Representative (GRP), or Page, for NBC Television Studios in Burbank, California. Many Pages were excited by the frequent showbiz interactions that were accessible and provided by a major TV network facility. Some found work within and outside of the industry. Others found their job only uncovered a depressing, even insulting Hollywood experience.

For me, it was the ultimate. By the time I arrived at NBC in the Big '80s, the Page position had grown into one of the most sought-after entry-level jobs in the entertainment field. Being a Page at this time involved running into Ricky Schroeder (then of NBC's *Silver Spoons*, later of ABC's *NYPD Blue*) or Boy George (who was working on one of the *Motown Summer Specials*), joking with Doc Severinsen (conductor of *The Tonight Show* band), studying the backstage workings of a *TV special* or going on a limo-run with one of the stars of NBC's *Hill Street Blues* or *Days of Our Lives*. It was a time before the network's expanding obsession with the *Law & Order* franchise and *Dateline*, the must-see super success of *Seinfeld, Frasier, Friends* and *Will & Grace*; it was the *Cosby Show* era of the company's initial super resurgence in popularity, when *Cheers* was merely hitting its peak.

I found myself on the set of *Family Ties*, *The Golden Girls* and *Wheel of Fortune*. I helped to coordinate an affiliates' convention, two press tours, five Bob Hope specials, *An All-Star Salute To President Dutch Reagan*, the *1984 Democratic Presidential Debates*, and the *1984 Emmy Awards*. I laughed with established comedians, lunched with network suits, hob-knobbed with celebrities, stuffed envelopes — and passed out tickets to *Scrabble* — all for a measly $5.20 an hour.

It's an experience I remember in-depth with *NBC & ME: My Life As A*

Page In a Book, in which I expose for the first time the behind-the-scenes shenanigans of my network tenure. Within these pages (every possible pun intended), I take you behind closed-doors, down inactive hallways, and inside TV's oldest web of intrigue (that's what we used to call television networks in the old days — webs). This book offers the fast-track, inside-scoop, close-up-look, and behind-the-scenes peek at my wannabe life with the so-called Peacock network — which, by the way, was the first broadcast television network to ignite the Page program.

Since 1933, NBC has offered what have now become historic tours of its facilities in Burbank, California, New York, and Chicago. Hundreds of thousands have paced through the studio gates and peered behind the scenes of various NBC shows over the years — all guided by NBC Pages — each of whom served as world guides to TV's initial broadcast net. Hundreds of young adults have been applying for the Page position every year in the seven decades since the studio commenced the GRP in New York, including famous former-Pages, such as:

Kate Jackson (of ABC's *Charlie's Angels*), Ken Howard (of CBS' *The White Shadow*), Richard Benjamin, Steve Allen (one of the original hosts of NBC's *Tonight Show*), Dave Garroway (original host of NBC's *Today Show*), Eva Marie Saint, Gordon MacRae, Efrem Zimbalist, Jr. (ABC's *The FBI*), Willard Scott (NBC's iconic *Today Show* weatherman, pre-Al Roker), Regis Philbin, Tex Antoine, Ted Koppel (ABC's *Nightline* host) and CBS-TV's *Captain Kangaroo* himself, the late Bob Keeshan (who as *Kangaroo*, kind of always looked like a Page).

There have also been several top network executives who are former Pages, such as the now infamous and former Disney/ABC high-roller Michael Eisner, and others who have risen through the ranks at NBC constituting a unique fraternity (*NBC Betamax?*) within the corporation.

In either case, *NBC & Me* is the first book to chronicle NBC's (or any other network's) infamous Page department. In doing so, this tome piggybacks on the optimum, full-fledged media buzz surrounding the professional, interpersonal, psychological, emotional, quite humorous and sometimes extremely scandalous antics surrounding an internship. (Can anyone say former Congressman Mark Foley and/or Former White House intern Monica Lewinsky, who is best remembered for her sexual liaison with former President Bill Clinton — and who recently received a Master's of Science degree in Social Psychology from the London School of Economics?)

NBC & ME also rides the skirt-tails of past or recent hit television shows like A&E's *Airline* (which was really *Pages on a Plane*), Andy Dick's *The Assistant*, and, of course, Donald Trump's and NBC's very own hit reality show, *The Apprentice* — as well as the success of NBC's mini-hit comedy, *30 Rock* (which features the Peacock net's former *Saturday Night Live* star/writer Tina Fey and offers periodic appearances by a character who just so happens to be a Page).

Sound like fun? Of course it does (especially since some of the names have been changed to protect the idiots).

So, come on — *let's all go there...*

CHAPTER 1

Gimme A Break

Let's all be there...

Or so went the commercial slogan for the campaign that NBC employed for its 1984-1985 TV season. At the time, the network was merely the *Mr. T*- breeding-ground for *The A-Team*, and home to no-hit wonders like *Manimal* and *The Misfits of Science* (starring a pre-*Friends* Courtney Cox, who I later attempted to romance).

For me, NBC was a doorway into the industry. As began the theme for *The Brady Bunch* (initially on ABC in 1969 and revisited by NBC in 1990 as *The Bradys* and again in 2000 as a behind-the-scenes TV-movie), *here's the story*:

I graduated with a B.A. in Theatre Arts from Nazareth College of Rochester, New York (my hometown) in the spring of 1983 and, like so many college grads (with or without a BA in Theatre Arts or Drama), I moved to Los Angeles to pursue my dreams. One of those dreams involved being an actor, preferably on a TV sitcom or daytime soap opera.

I also, of course, had this secret fantasy to play Erik Estrada's younger brother, who I named, Honch, as a replacement for his Ponch character on NBC's *CHiPs*. (You know — just like Cheryl Ladd had replaced Farrah Fawcett as her character's younger — and better built — sister on ABC's *Charlie's Angels*?) But since NBC had just since cancelled *CHiPs* (in the spring of 1983), and even though I once observed the show being filmed on Sunset Boulevard in the heart of Hollywood some six years before (during my first visit to Los Angeles in the spring of 1977), that dream was dead — at least by the fall of 1983. By that point, I just needed a place in which not only to live my dream, but just a place to live, period.

After a brief search, I ultimately found a studio apartment in the Brentwood/West Los Angeles area on what today is somewhat of a well-known street of dreams (and way too many nightmares): South Bundy Drive.

Fortunately, my initial L.A. apartment hunt transpired some ten years before Bundy Drive had become infamous for the controversial affairs of a certain former athlete in the guise of O.J. Simpson — who actually lived on *North* Bundy Drive. I was still pretty much safe, though I certainly didn't require O.J. to make ominous my stay on Bundy. In not so many words, I would have been much better off had I moved to the other side of the city.

I ended up subletting the apartment from a mysterious woman with whom the previous male tenant (who had recently died) was acquainted. The place was mine, if I wanted it. But I wasn't allowed to tell the landlord. Instead, I was instructed to send my rent check to the enigmatic woman, who in turn, was instructed to "take care of it."

I felt something was amiss. My spider senses were tingling. But I ignored them, mostly because I had reached a primary goal — again: a place to live and, and it was dirt cheap at $175.00 a month. Yet dirt cheap took on a double meaning once I actually stepped into the apartment — which was filthy — and which sorely needed what is known today as an *extreme makeover*. But the extensive amount of required home improvement effort ultimately became a good thing.

I was still smarting from a summer-love-gone-sour (I hate you, Sonya), and I figured that fixing up the disheveled apartment would have proved to be therapeutic — or would have at least helped me to establish a sense of independence. I'm not so sure if either of those goals panned out (I still hate you, Sonya), but I was willing to give it a shot. I really got in there, and scrubbed and painted, even ripped off ugly wallpaper from the bathroom wall. Unfortunately, during that latter trial and error period, some of the actual wall came off in the process. That's when I decided to forget the whole thing and hire professionals.

I opened the yellow pages, and telephoned a random painter. I was quoted a price of $150.00, which seemed fair. Some hours later, the painters arrived. They completed their work, and I immediately became dissatisfied with the job. So, I needed a break. Yet instead of a burger at McDonald's (which may have lead to my own French fry franchise), I attended a taping of NBC's *Family Ties*, a title of which later played prophetic for my soon-to-be-TV-network and me.

CHAPTER 2

The Ties That Found Me

I always thought *Family Ties* was a fun show. I admired the many talents of its star, Michael J. Fox, who played the program's central character, wiz-kid, Alex P. Keaton. During the sitcom's genesis, Fox was not envisioned as its focal point. The series was intended as a star-vehicle for Meredith Baxter-Birney, who played Fox's mother, Elyse, and who had previously starred with her husband David Birney in *Bridget Loves Bernie* (the groundbreaking CBS series from 1973 about a Catholic woman who marries a Jewish man and which, unfortunately, was cancelled after a few episodes).

When Fox auditioned for *Ties*, then-NBC entertainment president Brandon Tartikoff, who passed away in the early 1990s, labeled the actor as "too cocky," and originally cast another young thespian in the role. Tartikoff was later encouraged to run with Fox and, once *Ties* hit its stride, Baxter-Birney's talents were heavily outweighed.

The Keaton family, with Fox and Baxter-Birney in place, along with Justine Bateman (as Mallory, Alex's sister), Tina Yothers (Jennifer, the youngest sibling), and Michael Gross (Steve, the father), was now in for a visit from beyond the fourth wall. Here's how it all went down:

In October of 1983, I was standing in line for a *Ties* ticket, outside Paramount Studios on the trendy Melrose Avenue. I made the cut for a seat inside (which doesn't always happen), and was excited about the initial prospect of watching an episode of a TV sitcom being filmed, or in this case, taped. For years before, I had listened to the familiar on-air announcements:

"*All in the Family* was videotaped before a live audience."

"*Laverne and Shirley* was filmed before a live audience."

"*Happy Days* was filmed before a live audience" (at least in the show's latter years after it destroyed its initial focus and the quaint appeal of the

Cunningham family — and started to concentrate on the obnoxious involvement of Fonzie, played by the Emmy-winning and awesome Henry Winkler, who I later encounter at NBC's rear-lobby).

I was prepped, perched and psyched to view in person the *Ties* episode, which I soon learned involved Mallory's first day of college, and the intellectual Alex offering moral support. The segment was a fine outing, as both Bateman and Fox were in top form. Justine Bateman, I might add (and I just did) is sister to Jason Bateman, who was then battling for screen time with pre-tween Ricky Schroder on NBC's *Silver Spoons* (and who today is also known as one of the stars of the now-cancelled cult favorite *Arrested Development* — which aired on FOX — the network, not Fox, the *Ties* star).

But it's the interplay between Fox (the *Ties* star and not the network) and Bateman (the sister, and not the brother) in between takes, that proved more entertaining. Both actors were impressed enough with their talents to offer one another several pats on the back — literally. What's more, Fox, in between hugs, traveled several times off-stage to either study lines or visit the men's room with a severe case of... well, I'll leave that up to your imagination.

Yet it was outside the studio, in the parking lot — following the *Ties* taping — when the pace really increased. *My* pace anyway — because that's when I started walking to my car, and first took serious notice of the surrounding Pages assigned to assist the audience. When I was in line beforehand, I guess I didn't give too much thought to the Guest Relations Representatives. I was merely excited just to be in the *Ties* line and, as I said, to have made the cut to see any show, let alone such a great series like *Ties* (which would go on to become one of the small-screen's biggest sitcom classics).

Once outside, following the afterglow of viewing a TV sitcom in person, my mind was somewhat settled. I was able to focus on other things — like applying for a position as an NBC Page. "Now that would be a great job to have," I thought.

Little did I know that in moments I would meet someone very influential who would seal such a destiny, pave the way for my dream to come true — or at least, take the time out of his very busy life to talk to me. That's right — once I made it back to the parking lot at Paramount Studios, I met *Family Ties* creator and producer Gary David Goldberg, and actually had a conversation with him. "You have a great show there, Mr. Goldberg," I said (as if he needed to hear that personal review from me).

"Well, thank you," he replied in kind.

"This has to mean something," I began to think to myself. "Why would this big-time TV guy actually respond to one of my oh-so-cool-and-casual comments if it didn't somehow *mean something*? Did it mean that I was destined to be party to this crazy magic called Hollywood? Oh, give me a sign, God! Give me a sign!"

As I was more or less in the process of becoming mentally unstable, a nametag on some random Page-dude walking by would have to suffice (as a *sign*). "Excuse me," I said to this young man, who stopped to humor me. "Mr...uhm...Smith is it?"

"That's right," he replied. "But you can call me Horris."

"Oh, okay...uhm...Horris," I said. "Well, I would like to do what you're doing. But how would I go about....uhm...doing that?"

"It doesn't pay anything," Horris continued with mild exasperation, as though he heard the question a million times (which he probably did). "The hours suck, and the work isn't filled with all the glamour that you'd might expect."

"I'm sure it won't be easy," I responded, "but as you can see, I'm very, very willing to give it a shot."

Horris took a moment to assess the eager sanctioned one before him and then, with a measure of caution, inquired, "Okay...Do you have a piece of paper?"

"Yes, here...somewhere."

"Good. Call Eba Hawkins at NBC. She's the Director of Guest Relations..."

"You mean, *Pages*?"

"Yes...Pages. Her secretary's name is Karen Powers. She's a real nice person. Tell her you spoke with me, and that you would like to set up a general interview to become a Page."

"Eba Hawkins. Karen Powers. General interview. Got it. I mean I didn't *get it* yet," I giggled like a fool. "I mean, *got it* as in *I understand*."

Horris didn't really care if I understood anything because, by this time, he just wanted me to shut up. Unfortunately, for him, I babbled on. "Thanks a lot, Mr. Smith. I mean, Horris. I appreciate it. I really, really do."

"Yeah — well, okay," Horris said, as he walked away with a feeling that he may have just made a complete mistake in the offering of exclusive inside information.

No matter. I screamed "Yes!" and proceeded to do one of those silly air-jumps that people do after a positive accomplishment. My foot was in the door. Yet, unbeknownst to me, there were hundreds of other doors out there, accompanied by at least as many feet. So did I instead just insert my foot into my mouth?

I found out the answer two weeks later following a telephone call to Ms. Powers, and a subsequent interview with Ms. Hawkins. Hawkins was cordial, but intimidating. She was tall, had big hair, a raspy voice, and reminded me of a latter-day Lucille Ball. Despite it all, the meeting went well, and Eba seemed to like me. Though that was my perception, she didn't make said observations abundantly or urgently clear.

I waited another few weeks for a response, but heard nothing. Easter was around the corner, so I took off to Phoenix to visit relatives that weekend. Upon my return to Los Angeles on Monday morning, and just as I walked in my apartment door, the phone rang.

"Hello."

"Herbie J Pilato, please."

"This is he."

"Herbie J — this is NBC. How would you like to start your job as a Page on Monday?"

"I'll *be there*," I replied, echoing the network's aforementioned then-popular slogan.

CHAPTER 3

The NBC Parking Lot

Five days after that initial telephone conversation with NBC, I was inside my 1981 Buick Regal Limited (white outside/plush red velvet inside), waiting in the NBC parking lot in Burbank, California, the infamous city about which Johnny Carson had joked for years. Would I actually be dining in the equally infamous NBC Commissary? Or would I never eat lunch in this town again?

I didn't have time for the answers. I was late for work. So I leapt out of my car, and walked over to the Guest Relations booth on the other side of the studio where the NBC tour commenced — the same tour that I as, well…a tourist…had taken years before. I recalled visiting *The Tonight Show* set with other members of the tour group, and looking at *that couch* on the set, while the tour-guide babbled away about backdrops and lighting gels.

I would soon be one of the Pages steering NBC tours, walking backwards, and pointing out things like *Laugh-In's* famous *Fickled Finger of Fate*, or the dressing room that once housed the late Red Foxx (during *Sanford & Son's* historic reign). *I* would soon be the one to breeze through the studios where they taped *Chico and the Man*, *The Dean Martin Show* and all those dreadful *Roast* specials. *I* would soon be the one designated to explain why *Welcome Back, Kotter*, an ABC show, was once videotaped (and not filmed) at NBC's Burbank studios — a Hollywood lot that housed videotape facilities which, like other Hollywood studios, rents to sister studios for profit.

Would anyone care about these things? Did I, when I first took the NBC Tour as a layperson? Or, now that I was in Hollywood, was I only concerned with getting laid? Again, it didn't matter. I was hired for a job that I had waited to attain for more than six months. I gathered my thoughts, walked up to the Ticket Booth and introduced myself. The Page in the Booth (a place that I would soon learn was designated as the *hell hole*) buzzed me in. "I have arrived," I thought. "I was just buzzed into NBC."

Once in the Page Lounge (which featured a ceiling littered with the pinned nametags of former Pages), I was huddled together with six or seven other new Pages (there was a new class every other month or so). One of these new Pages was named Tony Pete.

Tony and I hit it off immediately, mostly because we discovered that we were both Libras and born on the very same day, October 9th (which also happens to be John Lennon's birthday) in the very same year (1960). Though I'm not sure if Tony shared my very same birth time (which was 6:58 PM).

He was tall (and still is) at 6'2", and I was short (and still am) at 5' 7". When standing next to one another, we looked like Ricardo Montalban and Hervé Villechaize, better known as Mr. Roark and Tattoo from *Fantasy Island*, a show that was then a big broadcast hit for rival network ABC. My New-York-State-beige-three-piece-suit-state-of-mind, most similar to that of Roark and Tattoo's, did not much help to deflect the similarities. As such, from thereon in, Tony referred to me as Herbé (with a b) — and I called him Mr. Dork.

It was a playful friendship, and proved insincere on Tony's part when, some years later, he became the head of Guest Relations for one of the big studios in Hollywood — and he didn't hire me when I needed a job.

The twad.

CHAPTER 4

Return to Mayberry

Though loyalty to Herbie J was not abundantly clear with Tony Pete, it was more clearly defined with other Pages. There was a wonderful dude in the guise of Mike Nannini, who was part of another class that was hired sometime after my group in May of 1984. But I must preface this memory with a flashback to October of 1983, when I attended an early screening of *Splash*, directed by former child/teen star Ron Howard.

Today, of course, Howard is known as the iconic feature film director of new big screen classics like *The Da Vinci Code* and *A Beautiful Mind*, and as the TV producer/director of recent small screen cult classics like FOX-TV's aforementioned and short-lived (but much-loved) *Arrested Development* (which Howard also narrated, and which featured the aforementioned Jason Bateman).

When I met Howard in the fall of 1983, he was best known for roles on two of television's most classic sitcoms: *The Andy Griffith Show* (CBS, 1960-1968) and *Happy Days* (ABC, 1973-1984). Howard's casting on *Griffith* followed his success at playing a five-year-old little Eddie in the 1963 feature *The Courtship of Eddie's Father* (which later became an ABC-TV series with Brandon Cruz in Howard's shoes). On *Griffith*, Howard was billed as little Ronnie Howard, playing little Opie Taylor, when he was just a mere pint-lad of 6-years-old. By the time *Happy Days* rocked around the clock at 8 PM on ABC, Tuesday nights, Howard was in his early-twenties, and starring as Richie Cunningham, the immortal 1950s TV teen (and sidekick to the previously mentioned Henry Winkler, who played Arthur *The Fonz* Fonzarelli, aka, Fonzie).

In October of 1983, Howard attended that early screening of *Splash*, a motion pictured he helmed following the success of his 1982 film, *Night*

Shift, and just prior to his massive movie hit *Cocoon* in 1985. *Splash* featured a young pre-Oscar-winning Tom Hanks (then-best-known from ABC's *Bosom Buddies*, ABC, 1980-84) and Daryl Hannah.

Truth be told, Ron — as Opie and Richie — was invited into my living room for the previous three decades. So, of course, when I saw him in person, I felt like I had known him and, also of course, I felt comfortable enough to say hello. Who wouldn't? Everyone in line for *Splash* that night probably felt like they had known little Ronnie Howard. What does anyone do when they see someone they know? They say hello. So, I said hello. Actually, I said, hi. "Hi, Ron," to be completely honest. That's right — I metaphorically stepped out of line and said, "Hi Ron" to Ron Howard. I was casual. I wasn't cruel. I was kind. I felt unworthy. But still, I said "Hi Ron" to Ron Howard.

Much to my (and hopefully your) pleasant surprise, Ron's response was amicable. He actually tipped his cap (which he had just started to wear due to his then new-receding hair line) and said "Hi" right back at me — and I thought that was really cool.

In fact, the evening continued to be cool — at least until a few seconds after I said "Hi" to Ron Howard. That's when someone else in line decided to turn up the heat. That's when some idiot in line decided to turn up the heat. A little back-story:

By this particular mid-October evening of 1983, Howard had made his now famous appearance on NBC's *Saturday Night Live* episode in which then-*Not-Ready-For-Prime-Time Player* Eddie Murphy had referred to him as *Opie Cunningham* (combining the names of Howard's two *Griffith/Days* characters into one fake moniker).

Sure enough, some big, tall, red-haired, freckle-faced goofball in line for *Splash* made a massive leap across the boundaries of good taste and yelled out, "Hey, look — it's Opie Cunningham! It's Opie Cunningham!"

I stood back a minute, and just looked at this guy who I thought resembled some *bizarro world* version of Opie-Cunningham-meets-Ted Koppel-and-Alfred-E.-Newman (the front cover model for *Mad Magazine*). "What a moron!" I said, point-blank, while shaking my head, and starring into the dead cool air of the October sky.

Flash-forward a few months to the spring of 1984 and back in the Page Lounge at NBC; that very same asshole was standing right in front of me. It was Mike Nannini, who just walked into the lounge as part of a new Page Class (and as a few paragraphs of a page in this book). After a few moments, I approached him and introduced myself. I told him how I remembered his face and stance from the entire *Splash*-Ron-Howard-*Opie* incident. Without skipping a beat, Mike laughed hysterically, we became the best of friends — and he turned out to be the farthest thing from a moron that I had ever met.

CHAPTER 5

The Star Treks Commence

Saying hi to Ron Howard that one fateful night at that special pre-screening of *Splash* in the Fall of 1983, and speaking with the frazzled *Family Ties* creator Gary David Goldberg on the Paramount lot (both encounters of which transpired months before I commenced work as a Page for NBC), were mere foreshadows to the number of star meetings that would take place during my reign inside (and outside) the Guest Relations Department at the Peacock Network. It was all a good balance. Periodic collisions with TV personalities proved to be the perfect antidote for slave wages and treacherous work conditions that went along with the challenging job of being an NBC Page.

Many of my colleagues and I likened it to boot camp. In a mere three weeks, we had to learn the history of NBC. That meant reaching back to the first NBC news show (*Meet the Press*), understanding the technical and somewhat boring underpins of a lighting gel, and perfecting the proper communication skills and poise it required to relay said information to visitors on the NBC tour — all within 45 minutes, while walking backwards, and for only $5.20 an hour. It was a learning process in the sincerest sense of the term.

Essentially, I was getting paid to attend graduate school. What I learned in my (contracted) 18-months as a Page was immeasurable. A good portion was also unnecessary. But it definitely was immeasurable, especially the fun parts — like doing limo-runs with the stars. Here's how it worked:

The network's press and publicity department matched Pages with celebrities to guide. A limousine company worked in liaison with NBC, and a driver was regularly scheduled to pick up the selected Page in Burbank. On very early mornings, the chauffeur arrived at the chosen Page's abode. In my particular case, that was my new (as in new to me) studio apartment on 17th Street and Wilshire in Santa Monica (to which I had moved from South Bundy Drive in West Los Angeles), before it became the Manhattan/Cannes of the West, before Pacific Park transformed into Disneyland by the Beach, and before the Third Street Promenade took over the universe.

Those with whom I drove back and forth to the airport, home and the studios, included stars like Conrad Bain, the father from the troubled set of NBC's *Diff'rent Strokes* sitcom and CBS' *Maude* (on which he played Bea *Golden Girls* Arthur's neighbor), soon-to-be megastar Michael J. Fox (fresh from my first encounter at a taping of *Family Ties*), actor Harry Anderson (who guest-starred on NBC's *Cheers* and later landed the lead on the network's *Night Court*), and Barbara Whinnery (part of the ensemble cast of NBC's esteemed *St. Elsewhere*).

Whinnery, in particular, was the kindest of all the stars I met. She was an extremely sweet woman, and talked fondly of her work on *Elsewhere*, which gave birth to the hit careers of people like Howie Mandel (host of NBC's prime-time game show, *Deal or No Deal*) and the Oscar-winning Denzel Washington. Whinnery even offered me some advice on acting; and how important it was to do theatrical showcases and plays in Los Angeles, mostly because the people in the audience usually included casting directors always on the look-out for new talent.

"That's how I get the job on *St. Elsewhere*," she told me. "One of the casting directors at NBC saw me in a play, locally, and called me in to audition."

However she got the part, Whinnery was a true pearl in what may sometimes be perceived as the land of real swine — and I will always remember her fondly.

CHAPTER 6

Miami's Nice & Vice

Another happy recall in the line of limo-run-ins with NBC personalities was my experience with Sandra Santiago. Santiago was the hot-on-all-levels co-star of NBC's then-mega-hit *Miami Vice*, which was transformed into a hit feature film in 2005 (starring Collin Farrell and Jamie Foxx as detectives James Sonny Crockett and Ricardo Tubbs, characters originally played by Don Johnson and Philip Michael Thomas on the TV series).

Like Barbara Whinnery before her, Sandra was a kind and gentle woman. We hit it off quite well, and we made certain to at least acknowledge one another at various NBC functions — that is, until her then-boyfriend put a stop to all the waving. But before that, Sandra and I were cool. She was always wonderful, and never was a problem-performer, unlike some people — such as one of her *Vice* co-stars. Not only was this particular co-star, who shall go nameless, on the press tour with Sandra, but he was also on the rag the night we picked him up, and required a swift kick in the ass.

To this day, I remain unsure as to what the heck was bugging him, but he got in the limo mad, stayed mad for the entire drive from the airport to his house, and treated me and the limo-driver like, well, shit.

All the while, the adorable Sandra Santiago was gazing over at me with her big brown eyes and saying things like, "Please forgive him. We've been traveling a lot on this press tour. He's just really tired."

Yeah — well, he was also really a moron — and I don't mean in a big-tall-funny-and-very-likable-Mike-Nannini-kind-of-way. "Please, Herbie," Sandra would continue. "Please try to understand."

"Okay, okay," I said. As if I had a choice. What was I gonna do? Yell back at him? Ask the limo driver to pull over so I could go a couple of rounds with one of the *Vice* squad? Then what? Get fired? Because this guy was a moron? Thankfully, we were scheduled to first deposit the male thespian to his home, before we dropped off Sandra.

In a very short while, which in reality, seemed like a very long time, we arrived at this particular actor's house. The limo parked near the curb, and the actor stepped out of the car. I was sitting in front, on the passenger side, next to the driver. I, too, then exited the vehicle. I walked around to the back of the car, opened the trunk, and reached for the actor's luggage. I handed him his belongings, longing to leave and assumed, "Thank God we're through with this idiot." But then he did something that really startled me. He grabbed my hand. "Oh, great," I thought. "Here we go…" I thought he was making a pass at me, and that the truth was out; that his anger somehow stemmed from his frustration with coming to terms with what may have been his true sexuality, which I had fashioned that he had been masking for years. In other words, I thought he was gay *(not that there's anything wrong with that)*, and that he couldn't deal with it, and that the rest of us had to suffer because of it. But, ah — no. That wasn't the case. Instead, the actor reached for my hand — and slipped me fifty bucks and apologized for his behavior over the last 90 minutes.

So, pretty much all that stuff about him, being a moron and everything? Yeah, well, that was a little harsh.

CHAPTER 7

The Night I Rode With Rider

Another star with whom I limo-ran was David Hasselhoff, then the future king of the NBC-turned-syndicated smash hit *Baywatch*... and today one of the controversial judges of NBC's talent(less?) show, *America's Got Talent*. At the time, he was merely the star of NBC's *Knight Rider*. On that big sci-fi hit of the '80s, Hasselhoff spent most of his on-air time conversing with a talking-car (voiced-over by William Daniels of NBC's *St. Elsewhere*, later of ABC's *Boy Meets World*). For the moment, he would be retrieved by a vocal cord-less limo at Los Angeles International Airport (LAX) — after he and his new bride returned from their honeymoon in Hawaii.

Meanwhile, the limo driver and myself were also required to pick up another man and his wife in the guise of Hasselhoff's managers, both of whom appeared in their mid-fifties or older. Yet, no matter their age, or otherwise: they just sure just loved David. "David this, David that. David, David, David!" That's all you heard from the minute I met them, to the second I dropped them off. They were so good at their job (of loving and protecting Hasselhoff), it was sickening. It really was.

That said, when we finally (finally!) arrived at the airport, David was alone. His wife had decided to remain in Hawaii, while he returned to Kitt (the talking car).

I am happy to report that, as we were strolling through LAX, Hasselhoff was quite courteous to his fans. To my surprise, so were his managers, as they so proved when one male fan approached them, instead of Hasselhoff. "I'd really like to be an actor," the man revealed, sounding a lot like me when I approached Horris Smith about being a Page. "How would I go about doing that?" the man continued. "With a lot of hard work," the wife-manager replied, impressing me in the process.

When that aspiring actor walked away, however, the wife-manager turned to her husband-business-partner and said, "You know something — I feel sorry for that kid. You really have to have *it* to make it in Hollywood. And he didn't. He just didn't have *it*."

Eventually, we all stepped into the limo, and Hasselhoff was still pleasant as could be, though his voice was about twenty octaves higher than what you hear on screen. I wondered, "Maybe he's real tired, and over-concerned about all the weight he's gained on the honeymoon?" Marriage, I guess, at the time, had agreed with him (because it's certainly arguing with him now).

Yet as we're driving, all you heard (again) was Hasselhoff's married, doting managers, saying, *David! David! David!* The poor guy could do nothing but take it in, until, suddenly a station wagon appeared in front of us. The back storage area was filled with young kids. That's when I said it. I don't know why I said it. But I said it. "If only those kids knew who was riding inside this limo."

"Oh, boy, you got that right," returned the married managers, almost in unison. Humble, kind, tired, and overweight David just bowed his head and smiled. Then, after we delivered Hasselhoff home, the limo traveled about another mile-and-a-half and we dropped-off his managers somewhere in Beverly Hills. They were proprietors of one of the older homes, still styled in ancient, decrepit stucco from the 1960s, landscaping and all. They uttered not one word since we left David at his doorstep. They were exhausted from talking. At least I thought they had to be — because I certainly was drained from hearing them speak. "Geez," I thought, "I don't know how David puts up with them." (Or if he still does?)

Thank God, Hasselhoff still *has it*!

CHAPTER 8

Fox Back In The Fold

A few weeks after my engagement with the David Hasselhoff clan, I was assigned to retrieve Michael J. Fox who today, of course, is such a valiant supporter of those stricken with Parkinson's disease (from which he also suffers). Due to the fact that I was motivated to be a Page via the set of *Family Ties*, I likened a limo-run with Fox as a life-comes-full-circle experience. And in a way, it became just that.

As with Hasselhoff, we (the limo driver and me) had to first retrieve Michael's representative. In this case, it was someone I'll call Judy, his West Hollywood publicist. We arrived at Judy's building, and I ran to fetch her, while the driver parked the limo. Her apartment was a mess. Photos of a various stars from TV and the movies trampled her living room wall and floor space, as did entertainment magazine articles upon articles. I wondered, "But don't these people (PR reps/agents/managers) ever rest?"

Judy reached for her briefcase, and we walked out to the limo. I was told we had to stop at Safeway's supermarket to pick up a six-pack of Moosehead beer for Michael, as the actor is a native of Canada, where Moosehead is brewed. Thus, it was his favorite beer (and I'm assuming it still is).

We soon arrived at Paramount Studios, where the actor enjoyed a wrap party for the 1984-1985 *Family Ties* season. Everyone was there: Justine Bateman, Meredith Baxter-Birney (nursing twins from David Birney, her co-star/husband from years before on the infamous, aforementioned and short-lived 1970s CBS sitcom, *Bridget Loves Birney*), and my old friend (wink, wink) *Ties* creator/producer Gary David Goldberg.

We allowed Michael to have a little fun, and Judy the publicist allowed me and the limo driver to join in on the festivities, which I thought was pretty cool. I was amazed to see Geena Davis, star of the NBC/Goldberg short-lived *Ties* sitcom spin-off, *Sara* (and years away from the film stardom of *Thelma and Louise*, *The Accidental Tourist* and the brief success of ABC's *Commander in Chief*). For some reason, I had the inkling that Davis, at nearly six feet tall, would want to dance with me, at barely five-feet-eight. So I garnered the courage and asked her, against the better and ultimately much wiser judgment of the limousine driver, who kept warning me, "Don't do it, dude. I'm telling ya'—you're gonna regret it. Don't do it!"

As I ignored the earnest pleas of this operator of long black cars, I found myself soon wishing that one hit me. After I queried Davis about a possible jig, she offered a polite head-shake, combined with one of those unpleasant and condescending closed-mouth smiles (which was partnered with those famous big lips of hers), looked *down*, and said, "I don't think so."

I then turned around and, a few seconds later, there sat my limo man, near the darkened empty audience seats of the *Family Ties* set. He had a severely annoying I-told-you-so look on his face, and pointed to the dance floor. We both then viewed Davis dancing with some jolly giant, as I sat like a little green pea with envy. In a moment, I composed myself, as much as any healthy New York Italian male could, watched the party rage on, and silently fumed inside. There I was, stood-up, pissed off and hoping that Davis and her dance-mate would both trip over their mammoth big legs (and lips).

Meanwhile, Judy the publicist notified us that we had approximately only fifteen minutes remaining to party. It was the summer of the first *Back to the Future* film and, if the movie was to be a success (which it certainly became, spawning two sequels), Michael had to get it in gear and hit the press circuit. So, within minutes, Fox jumped in the limo with his "I'm-a-busy-guy and almost-like-Alex P. Keaton-in-real-life" attitude, and we were off to the airport.

Upon arrival at LAX, the limo parked in front, and we hurried inside to board Fox on his flight to wherever. We headed for the ticket counter, and there was a slight flight delay. We made our way for one of the airport bars. Fox started to detail a recent visit to a children's hospital, when he walked into the rooms of various ill youngsters, and watched their faces light up. "They would actually get better," he told me.

I didn't doubt it. Overall, Fox behaved as unaffected as possible for being the big TV-turned-movie-star that he was in the process of becoming. We didn't really have that many common traits. But what we did share was significant. We're both nearly as short as Tattoo, and we both have the same middle initial. But let's be clear: I was actually born with my J (without a period), whereas Michael inserted his (with a period) later in life. Here's how it all went down:

When I was born, my father, originally named Pompeii — and who later changed his name to Herbie — decided to pass that latter moniker on down to me. But my Mom thought that would prove confusing. If she called out "Herbie," she argued, my father and I would have answered in unison. "So how about this," she went on to propose: "What if we attached little Herbie's middle initial to his first name and call him Herbie J, all in the same breath?"

Sounded good — and the decision was made. Herbie J was born, with me deciding later as an adult to drop the period (just to be different). Though, considering I was born with hair on my face and shoulders, I wasn't exactly the most attractive baby at Rochester's Highland Hospital on the day I was brought into this world (October 9th, 1960 at 5:58 PM). But you couldn't tell that to my dad. He was loyal to the end. So loyal, it hurt — somebody else.

At one point, one of the other fathers who were partially responsible for the birth of one of the other babies at Highland Hospital that day was standing next to my father near the incubator. Apparently, this man glanced at me through the window, nudged my dad, and said, "Hey, look at that ugly baby," unaware that the ugly baby and my father were related.

"You think so?" Dad responded. "Well, tell ya' what — that's *my* baby!" A huge brawl then ensued in the hospital corridor. Though I may have backed up the story a little too much with the last digression, I betcha' that never happened to Michael Fox, who only chose his own middle J initial (period and all) way after he was born.

As the Fox story goes: Michael J. admired the talents of veteran actor Michael J. Pollard (who may be best known to retro TV fans as Kim Darby's co-star in an episode of the original *Star Trek* series, entitled *Miri*, in which Pollard, as a freaked out leader of teen aliens, uttered classics lines like, "Bonk, bonk, on the head"). So in tribute to Pollard, Fox stole his middle initial.

Years later, when we two J's met, via NBC and LAX, Fox was generous with his conversation. We were sipping drinks at LAX, I with my ginger ale, he with his airport-purchased, favorite Moosehead beer. Near the end of our barroom repartee, the cocktail waitress walked over. I readied the funds NBC allocated me for expenses. Like only Michael J. Fox could (or Alex P. Keaton, for that matter), he scolded, "Don't you dare [hand flicking hair back] pay for these drinks!" I then informed Fox that NBC was footing the bill, and he retreated with, "Oh, well...that's different." Meanwhile, of course, his publicist Judy was smiling, and sounding an awful lot like David Hasselhoff's manager from a previous limo run with an NBC star. "Oh, Michael," she told Fox, "you're faaabbuulouss! Just faabbuulouss!" She actually said that. No lie.

Some twenty minutes later, Fox repaid the remark by walking behind her in the airport and blurting out, "Whoa! Judy, babe...you've got a great ass!"

Yet before all of this transpired, I opened my mouth (again, when maybe I shouldn't have), and said "Uhm, Mr. Fox?"

"Please…call me Michael."

"Okay, then…Michael…Do you mind if I say something?'

"Shoot."

"I really believe that you have done a lot for short people."

"Wow! Really! Wow, man. Thank you."

Though I was kidding, Fox was not and, years later, due to his charitable activism for Parkinson's disease, he proved himself to be the superior J (with or without a period).

CHAPTER 9

AirCourt '84

Many of you may recall this near-international incident from early 2007: According to *The Honolulu Advertiser*, film from ABC's hit show *Lost*, produced in Hawaii, was ruined when security employees at the Honolulu International Airport accidentally X-rayed the film's canisters despite warning labels asking them not to do so. As a result, the show's crew had to re-shoot the…uhm…*lost* sequences because there were no copies. "This is the first time anything like that happened," Film Commissioner Donne Dawson told the *Advertiser*.

That wasn't exactly true. Decades before, following my NBC limo Fox trot with Michael J., performer Harry Anderson was next on the list of my run-ins (*ruins?*) from celebrity homes to LAX, during which a very similar and unfortunate *Lost*-film-like incident transpired. Anderson, an accomplished magician, would later star in the mid-1990s CBS sitcom, *Dave's World*, based on the exploits of real-life humorist Dave Berry. But when I met him in 1984, Anderson was known as the former stand-up comic/magic-man who sat in the center chair of NBC's judicial humor hit, *Night Court* (after making a rousing guest appearance on *Cheers*).

As celebrities go, Anderson, like Michael J. Fox, was sincere, approachable, and cordial. That all changed, however, right before he took flight — when I insisted on hauling his luggage through the airport's tracking conveyer belt, and he lunged for a petite pouch. "No!" he objected with somewhat (but not too much) of a civil tone. "I'll take care of that one." He started to scribble something in a notebook. I grabbed my chance, reached for the guarded secluded satchel that was around his shoulder, and shoved it through the conveyer. I was hell-bent on impressing this guy with that famous NBC Page courtesy. Instead, he almost *bended* me. "Oh, guy!" he squealed. "No! No!

No! What did you do?! What did you do?!!"

Apparently, there was some form of disruption, similar to what had transpired with the *Lost* Hawaiian film in 2007: as the LAX airport terminal's infrared detecting device had erased months of hard work from the portable automated computer discs that Anderson placed in that small bag. But, hey, it was only the '80s. What did I know? What the heck was a TV actor doing with a computer anyway? And wait a minute: Anderson's a magician, right? Maybe he himself was actually responsible for making all of that disc data disappear? Yeah — that was the ticket: he was just *hatin'* on me to cover up his own guffaw.

Despite all the agitation, manufactured or sincere, Anderson ultimately composed himself. "Look, kid," he said, "it's been very nice meeting you. You're a very good Page. You did a great job. Give my best to everyone at NBC, would ya'?" And with that, he stormed through airport security.

"Mr. Anderson? Harry?! Judge?!! Sir??!! Houdini???!!!"

But no reply. He just kept on walking. Some months later, however, I observed Anderson and Michael J. Fox embrace at an NBC press party like they were long-lost brothers (that whole *NBC* family thing; as Fox had made a pre-*Family Ties* guest appearance on Anderson's *Night Court* during which they first became friends). Michael was as melodramatic as ever. "Hey, Harry," he shouted. "What's happening, man? You look fantastic! What's the word?!"

From there on, all I could envision was this dreadful conversation taking place:

Anderson: "Well, if you really want to know...You see that Page over there?"

Fox: "Oh, yeah...Herbie J."

Anderson: "You actually know that guy?"

Fox: "What do you mean? Herbie J's cool."

Anderson: "You wouldn't say that if he shoved your bags through the airport security conveyer and erased all your computer discs."

Fox: "Herbie J? Naw. No way. We share the same middle initial, and he thinks I've really done a lot for short people."

CHAPTER 10

The Golden Girls

Years before I become a Page, my time with NBC was foreshadowed in a celebrity brush with Bea Arthur, best remembered as TV's iconic *Maude* (CBS, 1972 to 1978), and soon to be recalled to fame as one of NBC's *Golden Girls*. I fist met Arthur in 1982, when she was starring in *Amanda's* (a.k.a. *Amanda's By The Sea*), a failed ABC series that was a cross between the BBC's *Faulty Towers* and CBS's *Newhart*. Here's what happened:

I was walking along Wilshire Boulevard in Santa Monica (past the scrumptious, now defunct Polly's Pies) when, all of a sudden, I heard this distinctly familiar voice. I turned, and there was Arthur, tall and raspy-voiced (in a Lucille-Ball-esque-Eba-Hawkins kind-of-way), walking with a middle-aged man who I only assumed to be her manager. I grew up on *Maude* (when I wasn't watching *Happy Days*), and though I never fully understood some of the more issue-oriented episodes of that groundbreaking series (like the earth-shattering abortion episode), I was not now about to pass up the opportunity to say hello to its iconic star (just as I would say hello to Ron Howard approximately one year later at the *Splash* debut).

Either way, I had to say something to Arthur. So I stopped Bea in her tracks, told her how much I enjoyed her work (yada, yada, yada), and wished her well with her new *Amanda's* series. She responded pleasantly enough, and then thanked me on my way.

The next time I met up with the actress, it was a completely different story — and series. It was 1985, and I was in my fourteenth month as a Page. Not only was I periodically assigned to join other Pages in ushering the audience for *The Golden Girls* (then fast becoming one of NBC's biggest Saturday night draws, toppling ABC's *The Love Boat* into cancellation), I was also supposed to escort each of the *Girls* from their respective limos to the press room, one by one, for that year's press tour. I was there to personally meet and greet Arthur, as well as Betty White, Rue McClanahan, and the lesser-known Estelle Getty (who would soon commence to steal many a *Golden* scene, much to the dismay of her then-much-better-known co-stars).

This time, Bea was terribly insecure (very unlike her *Girls* character, Dorothy Zbornak, or Maude Findlay for that matter), Rue was confident (just like her *Girls* guise, Blanche Devereaux), and Betty was very sweet (but not stupid like Rose Nylund, her *Girls* persona). Estelle, simply in awe of her surroundings, was the least known of the *Golden* quartet and, after years on the stage and in bit parts on the big screen, she was experiencing her first weekly stint in a prominent role on television as Sophia Petrillo, the very senior, cranky and stroke-inflicted mother to Arthur's Dorothy.

Getty was so stunned by her new position, that when her manager commented on how much I allegedly looked like her nephew, Phil, she turned to me and said, "Oh, hi Phil! How are you?!"

"No, Estelle," her manager clarified. "He only looks like Phil."

"Oh."

Meanwhile, Bea had clearly not remembered me from our Polly's Pies days, so I moved on. A few weeks later, however, I and another Page, Gretchen Harris, who became my good friend (and who today goes by the married name of Gretchen Harris Keskeys, and who has penned the foreword to this book) were hired as audience fillers for an NBC on-air special promoting the season. Fate took its hand, and Gretchen and I were randomly seated at a table with the *Golden* ladies. As the evening progressed, Rue and Estelle exited early, leaving me and my fellow Page at the table with Betty, Bea, and two empty chairs. So I struck up a conversation. "You know," I said to Betty and Bea, as Gretchen looked on, "you both are so adept at comedy, I bet if either of you said as simple a word as tomato, it would sound hysterical." As if they (like *Family Ties* creator Gary David Goldberg before them) needed to hear any confirmation of their talent from the likes of me.

Still, Betty, without missing a beat, turned to Bea and in a second to me, and asked, "Should we try?" As Bea then dragged madly away on her cigarette, she and Betty readied to exit in a huff (and a puff). Apparently, both were disgusted with the mistreatment of an animal during a skit for the show. At one point, White, a legendary animal advocate, turned to Bea and asked, "Shall we leave now?"

"Let's," Bea replied. "We don't need to sit through this shit!"

I would not see Bea again until a few months later — in a post-Page moment. Flashforward to 1986:

I was now working as an *extra* (or *atmosphere player*) on several television shows, including daytime soap operas like ABC's *General Hospital* and CBS'

The Bold and the Beautiful, and primetime sitcoms, like…that's right — *The Golden Girls*. By this time, I noticed that each of the *Girls* had changed, due to their unstoppable *Golden* fame. Betty and Rue were cordial enough. But when I first met Estelle, she had them all beat, and was the nicest woman in the world, minus even one ounce of Hollywood affectation. Yet in 1986 — a mere year after her *Golden* debut, Getty refused to remember or even acknowledge me. "Oh, come on, Estelle," I wanted to say, "It's me — your nephew? Phil…?"

Bea, on the other hand, had been staring at me all day. At first I thought that maybe she did indeed remember me from our Polly's Pies days. Or maybe she just plain liked me. Or maybe, somehow, she was going to be the one responsible for my big break (via one night with Bea Arthur).

None of the above. As it turned out, Bea instructed the show's assistant director (AD) to stop tape, and had me accosted for — da-da-da-dum — chewing gum. Arthur actually approached the AD, and whispered in his ear, while glancing in my direction. Seconds later, and with the look and tone of an elementary school principal, the AD gathered the small band of extras, which included me, and asked, point blank, "Okay, who has the gum?" Everyone looked at one another, and I gradually began to raise my hand.

"I do," I said, feeling like I had just indeed been reprimanded by Sister Ann Meanie Face. "Me. I have the gum."

"Well, would you please get rid of it?" the AD demanded.

"Uhm…sure," I replied, with my head, bowed, as I walked to the nearest trash.

I had just been busted by a *Girl* for some Chiclets. What could be worse, right?

Years later, I found out, while at the Tex Mex restaurant in Pacific Palisades, when I encountered Bea once more, this time with former *Maude* co-star Conrad Bain. On *Maude*, Bain played Dr. Arthur Harmon, who was married to Vivian, portrayed by Bea's *Golden* co-star, Rue McClanahan. As fate continued to conduct its evil scheme, I remembered how Conrad, then TV dad to Gary Coleman on *Diff'rent Strokes*, one of NBC's massive '80s hits, was one of my first limo-runs for NBC. Though *Strokes* was winding down by then, and would soon move to ABC for its final season, Bain was quite cordial, and spoke frankly about his former co-stars, from both *Maude* and *Strokes*. We discussed people like McClanahan, actor Bill Macy, who played Maude's husband, Walter, and Adrienne Barbeau, the latter of whom portrayed Maude's daughter — and who, according to Bain, was happily married to king horror feature film director, John Carpenter (*The Fog*, *Halloween*). Yet, Bain was mostly concerned about Coleman, who was struggling with health and legal issues. We spoke, too, of course, about Bea — and how different she looked with her nose job, slight face-lift, and healthy weight loss since their days together on *Maude*. "An actor loses personal character when they [go under the knife] to make themselves look too pretty," Bain said.

Observing Bea and Bain — as I awakened at Tex Mex in 1986 from this memory blur of 1984, my date — a fellow Pagette named Susie Lynn (who I will now introduce as the one true love of my life as a Page, for 18 months and somewhat beyond), was being hit-on by none other than actor Robert Carradine (brother to David Carradine, the iconic star of classic TV's *Kung Fu* — for which I would later write two companion books). At the time, Robert was hot with a hit-streak of *Revenge of the Nerd* movies, but now he was acting like one in reality. I managed to pull Susie Lynn away from him, as I continued to observe Bea and Bain, both of whom were leaving in her big black BMW. I couldn't help but notice how suited Bea was to that vehicle.

You know how, after a fashion, some people begin to look like their pets? Apparently, that rule also goes for autos. In a split-second, I flashed-back to the Sunset-Gower Studios in Hollywood, where Bea taped *The Golden Girls* (which later moved to Ren-Mar Studios due to a new contract with NBC). I remembered the *Golden* line-up of star-cars in the Sunset-Gower parking lot. Bea helmed the aforementioned big black BMW. Rue McClanahan guided a tan four-door Mercedes sedan. Betty White toured with a mint-green Cadillac Seville, and Estelle Getty drove a teeny, tiny little Chevette.

Somehow, it all fit.

CHAPTER 11

The Big Events

Beyond *The Golden Girls* press parties, I helped to coordinate many glamorous, up-scale gatherings and major events connected with NBC from 1984 to 1985, including: *The Democratic Debates* (with Jesse Jackson and Walter Mondale), *The Emmy Awards* and *An All-Star Salute To President Dutch Reagan*. The *Dutch* party, in particular, was attended by the likes of Robert Wagner (once the star of NBC's 1960s cult classic, *It Takes A Thief*), Clint Eastwood (who guest-starred in an early episode of NBC's *McCloud* in 1968), President Reagan, Ted Danson (star of NBC's then super-hit *Cheers*), Vicki Lawrence (of CBS' *The Carol Burnett Show* that spun-off into *Mama's Family*, the first season of which was on NBC), and John Forsythe and Linda Evans (Blake and Krystle Carrington, from ABC's *Dynasty*, no less).

The Democratic Debates with Jesse Jackson and Walter Mondale proved to be an interesting gig for me. I got to play "tough security guard." Trust me: as a little Italian Page wearing a uniform reminiscent of an airline steward, that's not exactly an easy thing to do. But I did it — and it was great fun. That is to say, I usually enjoyed the rush of power that came along with making sure that all the "apples and oranges" were properly in line during tapings of everyday events like *The New Let's Make A Deal*. And I do mean apples and oranges, somewhat literally, as in the gear in which *Deal* contestants many times arrived.

With the *Democratic Debates*, however, I completely embraced the opportunity to boss around dignitaries of every kind, so much so that I impressed the Head of Security from one of the government organizations associated with the United States (The CIA? The FBI? The FCC? *The A-Team?*) that was assigned to work with the Pages. "We gotta' hire this guy," he said, in reference to me, as he turned to a few other members of his team.

I just stood there with an awe shucks look on my face, and everything went swimmingly from there, or at least until I was forced to scold the conservative representatives from *The Christian Science Monitor* (CSM). Then everything good, kinda-sorta turned bad — on several levels. The CSM group had made a special bus trip to the studio just for the Debates. Once off the bus, the band was not too concerned with remaining in line. As a result, I had little choice. I was forced to take the bull by the horns. Or at least, throw around some of that bull for which I had by then become famous. In full control-freak mode, I went on to admonish the group. "Ok," I said, "all you *Christian Science Monitors* better make sure you keep a straight line."

Boy, did that remark (intended only with humor) rub them so completely the wrong way. They actually became rowdy. They assumed I was addressing them condescendingly as *Christian Science Monitors*, and I was merely attempting to tell them what to do with a smile, and to make them smile. But — ah — no. It didn't turn out that way. Since I was and remain on the lookout for a smooth path to Heaven, I backed off, and thought to save any continued debates for when I hopefully one day appear before St. Peter at the Pearly Gates.

CHAPTER 12

I Dreamt Of Jeannie

Life as a Page lightened up a bit with the commencement of the 1984 Emmy Awards, which were held at the Santa Monica Civic Auditorium. By the time this major industry ceremony approached, I was taken off line duty, and assigned inside to hold the clipboard to mark off the names of those VIPS who passed through my detecting eyes. Indeed, it was my turn to hold the big clipboard. That is to say, we were talking power with a capital P. How cool was it that I actually had the kind of leverage to clear such distinguished individuals like Placido Domingo and Barbara Eden, the latter of whom was to be followed by none other than her former *I Dream Of Jeannie* co-star-turned-*Dallas* legend, Larry Hagman.

I remember the Eden/Hagman incident as clear and loud as a bell, even though I silently screamed with adoring excitement upon my Eden encounter. "There's Jeannie! There's Jeannie! There's Jeannie!" Then, upon observing Hagman, I just plain freaked-out. "No. No. No. It can't be. Major Nelson is right behind Jeannie. Where am I? Do I really exist? Am I really here? Blink the two of us away, Jeannie! Blink the two of us, away!"

Something magical transpired when Eden, then approximately 55-years-old (and still looking perfect), walked in the door. I checked off her name on the board, and she just looked at me (then only 23) with, dare I say, not a blink, but with a twinkle in her eye. "Oh, only if you were about 30 years older," her eyes seemed to have pined.

To my chagrin, all of that was altered after everyone was seated, and Eden exited the auditorium, lost and looking for answers. "Looking for love?" I thought…I hoped. "Looking for me?" As I stood there in the lobby, in my Page uniform, with again, the appeal of a grounded airline steward (with no plane to catch — and certainly with little money to purchase a ticket), I caught Eden glancing my way. "This is it!" I continued in self-conversation. "She's gonna hit on me. Jeannie's gonna hit on. She's gonna start calling me Master, and everything. It's the ultimate fantasy, the ultimate dream come true (next to sleeping with Samantha from *Bewitched*, of course)."

Eden's feet started towards me. My heart began to beat. She was getting closer. Closer. Closer. "Excuse, me," she then blurted, with those eyes, still twinkling. "Could you please point me to the bathroom?"

"I love you, too..." THUD. I'm halted in my tracks. "Huh...??!!"

There I was, ready and waiting to rendezvous on a magic carpet ride with one of TV's most beautiful magic mavens, and all she wanted was directions to the loo.

"Oh, sure," I said, wilted with rosacea-inducing shame, "...it's around to the right." Then, as Eden walked away, I watched with melancholy, as her eye-twinkle allegedly became — drum roll please... a tinkle.

CHAPTER 13

I Remember Mama

The All-Star Salute To President Dutch Reagan was a major event that was taped on the NBC studio lot in Burbank. Everyone who was anyone (at the time) was there. At one point, you would see President Regan walking beside Frank Sinatra and Sean Connery (the one and only true *James Bond*). Other times, you would see people like actress/one-time-hit-songstress Vicki Lawrence (*The Night The Lights Went Out In Georgia*).

I soon observed the former CBS/*Carol Burnett Show* star and her husband chatting away about the new syndicated version of the short-lived NBC sitcom *Mama's Family*, which was a spin-off of Vicky's famous *Burnett Show* character. *Family* had just completed a very-poorly-rated first season run on NBC, which for the most part, was then stealing away many CBS stars for its own sitcom purposes. Bea Arthur, Betty White and Rue McClanahan, then starring on NBC's *The Golden Girls*, hailed from *Maude* (Bea and Rue, CBS, 1972-78) and *The Mary Tyler Moore Show* (Betty, CBS, 1970-77). So there was already bad-blood in the air. There was also no place left to take *Mama* (besides ABC and PBS, who must have just said no) except straight into syndication. Even Lawrence herself was startled, as she stood and listened to her husband make the potential-for-rerun revelation to the press. "Can they do that?" she asked with regards to the *Mama* switch from network to first-run syndication. "Yes," her husband nodded as he fielded questions from the press-arazzi.

Meanwhile, Vicki and I, though sharing no relationship whatsoever (beyond the fact that, back in eighth grade, I absolutely friggin' loved *The Night The Lights Went Out In Georgia*) were both shocked at the news. I couldn't believe what I was hearing because *Mama's Family* was such a dreadful show. Vicki couldn't believe what she was hearing because she probably thought the same thing: that it was impossible for a major network's once-dead less-than-mediocre series to find new life anywhere else, let alone in first-run syndication (which was a somewhat sparse pre-mainstream/cable mass-market at the time, sprinkled with fare like *Small Wonder*).

Frankly, it was a miracle that *Mama* was ever spun-off into a regular show in the first place — as it failed to work, creatively, on so many levels. Though this first full-fledged series edition of *Mama* appeared on NBC, it was videotaped at the CBS studios. Remember now: the networks rent out studio space to one another many times for convenience, and mostly for profit (and certainly not because they like it each other). Those producers involved with *Mama* (including former *Burnett* show-runner and former Burnett spouse Joe Hamilton) more than likely selected the CBS studios because that's where the original *Mama* skits were developed and taped (in the mid-to-late 1970s).

But nuts, as Mama might say, what a mistake! Many of the NBC-*Mama* segments were embarrassingly presented with the look and feel of a high school production (and I don't mean by Disney), complete with major reverb in the sound department and sophomoric staging. Such unprofessional distractions occurred not only because the episodes were produced at CBS Television City, but because they were also executed (or should have been *executed*, if you know what I mean) on the same exact sound-stage where the *Burnett* show taped.

Taping a sitcom on what was once a variety-show stage was and remains a massive no-no, and where *Mama* was concerned, it proved that lightning wouldn't strike twice. That first NBC season of *Mama's Family* may have had a *Honeymooners*-esque feel to it (and that's where Hamilton and company may have been attempting to take it). But that type of sit-comedy went out with the bathwater (and the tarnished kitchen sink) when Jackie Gleason's latter-day skits were cancelled along with his CBS variety show in the spring of 1974.

Today, of course, reruns of *Mama's Family* are a huge hit on the i network. So, what do I know, right?

Oh — and I almost forgot to mention that Jesse Gomez — the mother of all Page supervisors — was the spitting image of the actress who starred in NBC's classic series, *I Remember Mama*. So, since I was addressing Vicki Lawrence and *Mama's Family*, well, I just figured I'd kill two *Mamas* with one stone, and somehow combine the reference to both shows into the title for this chapter.

Pretty good, uh…?

CHAPTER 14

Krystle Blue Persuasion

Who would have thought we'd be talking about an ABC show so much in a book about NBC (and me). But that just goes to prove the incestuous connection within the entertainment industry. Other times, you were lucky to view the cast of *Dynasty*, including the likes of aforementioned John Forsythe and Linda Evans who, along with Joan Collins, took the co-leads on the very popular ABC show (which contributed to the self-absorption of the American mainstream in my beloved big '80s era).

Yet, years before *Dynasty* debuted (in 1981), Evans was best known as Audra Barkley on *The Big Valley*, starring alongside the legendary likes of Barbara Stanwyck and Lee Majors (who would later go on to become *The Six Million Dollar Man* for ABC from 1973-78, which I would chronicle in *The Bionic Book*, along with super-sister series, *The Bionic Woman*, which in turn, NBC would reconfigure for the fall of 2007). Sometime after Forsythe failed on TV with something called *To Rome With Love* (a kind of European knock-off of *Family Affair*), he hit the vocal-only TV big-time as the voice of Charlie on the ABC/Aaron Spelling super-sleuth hit *Charlie's Angels*. (*Angels* was a retread of the ABC/Spelling police-beat series *The Rookies*, which was itself a redo of the ABC/Spelling hippie-cop show *The Mod Squad*, all three on which featured a guest-star appearance by Sammy Davis, Jr. — who was an NBC staple on various variety shows and specials).

Here now, at the *All-Star Salute To President Dutch Reagan*, were Forsythe and Evans encountering Herbie J the Page. No one needed to alert the media (as pretty much everybody was already there), and this time my assignment had little to do with me keeping the audience "in line" or having to cross reference or cross off any names that may or may not have appeared on any list on any clipboard that I may or may not have been holding. No.

This time, I was assigned to open the car/limo doors to the stars as they exited their behemoth black-mobiles — and it was my jaw dropping encounter with Evans, in particular, that proved most memorable.

It was an especially cold afternoon on that November day in 1985 during the pre-taping moments of the *All-Star Salute To Reagan*. As Evans' limo approached the red carpet drop off, near to where I was assigned frequent door-reach duty, I remember shaking and shuttering in the bitter air, with my big white teeth clicking and chattering. When Evans' limo came to a halt, I reached for its door and, as per my assignment, waited for Evans to exit. But there was some kind of delay. So I peeked inside the vehicle to find out why, and what to my wondering eyes would appear but a beautiful vision of a TV star with nary a tear.

Okay, so maybe it wasn't all that Frank Capra. But my initial vision of Evans was glorious — and startling: Prince would have been proud, as I didn't have to watch *Dynasty*, to see her attitude, because she had none. Evans was as down to earth as they came, despite the fact that she was all decked out in light blue and white, and surrounded by royal blue, rich Corinthian leather seating (that surely was left over from those late 1970s-early-1980s Chrysler Cordoba TV and print ads that featured *Fantasy Island* star — and my early wardrobe consultant — Ricardo Montalban). Though, I must say, as I continued to gaze at Evans, I could almost hear the *Dynasty* theme music playing in the frigid air: "Da-da-da — DA — da da-da..."

After the music subsided in my head, Krystle, uh, I mean, Linda — did something ever so sweet and real, I just wanted to eat her up right there and then (get your mind out of the gutter; I don't mean it in *that* way). Because Evans was feeling the slightly bitter breeze of the now-near-evening November air, she turned to what I believe was her assistant in the vehicle and politely inquired, "Should I bring my sweater?"

My heart stopped. How could Blake, er, I mean, John Forsythe, ever choose Alexis, er I mean Joan Collins over Krystle, er I mean Linda?

"Should she bring her sweater?!" How cute is that?! Linda Evans shivered and got cold and everything. She wasn't at all like the Krystle-Carrington-beating-Alexis-Carrington-to-a-pulp-tough-as-nails-chick. Shoot, she wasn't even the horse-riding-platinum-blonde-stiff-haired-cowgirl-in-the-guise-of-Audra-Barkley from *The Big Valley*. Evans was a real-life/live-person who got real-life/live-cold just like the real-life/live-rest-of-us. This proved to be a defining moment in my observational world of TV stardom. It changed my life forever. It gave me hope. It made me think that maybe there really are some "good ones" out there.

CHAPTER 15

Pain Jane

Unfortunately, the memory of my awesome brush with Linda Evans and her fame would soon be clouded by the harsh-surreality of meeting one Ms. Jane Seymour at the Hall of Fame Awards.

In addition to the *All-Star Salute To President Dutch Reagan*, the next big event that I helped to coordinate at NBC was the *Fame* affair, which was attended by the likes of Seymour, among others. Some eight years later, Miss Jane (not to be confused with the skinny and all-too likable character of the same name played by the late, great Nancy Kulp on the CBS long-running hit, *The Beverly Hillbillies*), Seymour would become best known as TV's *Dr. Quinn, Medicine Woman*, and a periodic guest star on shows like Smallville and *How I Met Your Mother*. She also recently enjoyed a resurgence in popularity as one of the stars of ABC's super-popular reality entertainment series, *Dancing With The Stars*. When I met her, she was merely the queen of TV-movies and mini-series, a spoiled daughter of some rich physician, and ultimately, a pain in my ass.

Before the *Hall of Fame* show commenced (at the Santa Monica Civic Auditorium), Seymour was standing in the lobby of the theatre, surrounded in a circle of stars, including Donna Mills, then the huge attraction of *Knots Landing* on CBS. Both tiny in stature, Jane and Donna were no more than 5'7" — in heels.

At one point, the lobby lights commenced flashing, and the event was about to begin. I was the Page assigned to tell everyone to return to his or her seats. Jane, Donna and other lady stars were ignoring my calls. Donna was polite, but little Miss Seymour was playing petty. Upon hearing my request to find her seat, she turned to me, read my nametag, and said with a sarcastic tone, "Okay — *Herr-beee!*"

I pouted, and thought, "What is it about these nametags?" Apparently, I would find out during my assignment on *Donahue*!

CHAPTER 16

Donahue!

An extremely challenging portion of being a Page was herding in the audiences for various special shows like *Donahue!*, the latter of which usually taped in New York.

For one week in 1985, the monumental syndicated TV talk show taped a number of unique segments at NBC's Burbank facilities. *Donahue!*, of course, was hosted by the charismatic Phil Donahue (who met Marlo *That Girl* Thomas — his wife of more than twenty years, when she made a guest appearance on his show). To accommodate the large audience, these particular episodes of the show utilized approximately one thousand people in Studio 4, which was regularly employed for game shows and variety specials. The NBC Page program was considered one of the finest in network public relations, mainly because of its organized seating procedures. An Outside-Page-In-Charge (OIC), and other detonated positions were assigned. The system was based upon rules that were set forth by the Burbank County Fire Marshall. A first-come/first-serve agenda lessened the possibilities of mass hysteria on entrance or exit of the studio, before and after the taping of a particular program, and yada, yada, yada.

Anyway, the *Donahue!* production staff, one female producer in particular who shall remain nameless, and to whom I will refer as She-Ra, had an alternate vision. When their audience began to enter the studio for the first of fourteen tapings (they produced two shows a day), all seemed tranquil. The audience was calmly escorted in, with the Pages, shining with integrity. Suddenly, She-Ra decided that life was not moving fast enough for her, or at least in the direction she had intended. I was the OIC and she approached me with her beef. "We need these people in here, now!" She-Ra demanded.

"Look," I said, tersely, "we have a certain way of filling a studio that's based upon laws instituted by the Fire Marsh..."

She-Ra cut me off. "No," she said, "...you look. If you don't get these people in here right now, as fast as you can, I'm gonna get on this here microphone and embarrass the hell out of you!"

"Nice," I thought, "the producer of *Donahue!*, a show that allegedly services the plight of common humanity, is making threats" (much more intensely and mean-spiritedly than Jane Seymour, I might add, though not as passive-aggressively).

She-Ra went on to scream directions to the audience through the microphone: "Okay, people, find a seat!" As the responding gatherers went wild, She-Ra turned to me and said, "The most important part of this show is the audience. If they're not happy with their seats, then it doesn't make for a good *Donahue!*. Got it?"

"Got it."

Witch.

CHAPTER 17

Law & Order

When I first started working at NBC, management, or at least the sub-management, was pretty hostile towards me. So, the whole *Donahue!* thing with She-Ra was kind of familiar territory for me at the time. More times than not, many of my Page peers and supervisors would take things much too seriously. When it came down to brass tacks, it was their own insecurity about their own position. Isn't that always the case with bullies? Case in point:

It was the fall of 1985. The major Fall Press Party for NBC's then new lineup was in gear, and that meant major promotions were in line for long-popular sitcoms such as *Gimme A Break*, *The Facts of Life* and *Silver Spoons*, as well as for new TV-movies, like *Two Fathers: Justice for The Innocent*, the latter of which featured the odd pairing of Robert Conrad and George Hamilton. Conrad had starred in two hit TV shows: *Wild, Wild West*, which aired on CBS from 1965 to 1970, and *Baa Baa Black Sheep*, which aired on NBC from 1976 to 1978. He also starred on two very short-lived shows: ABC's *Assignment: Vienna* and NBC's *A Man Called Sloan*, both of which attempted to ride and mimic the ever-popular *James Bond* spy-popularity. Hamilton, on the other hand, had not really had a hit anything for years, and was ultimately best known for his mere tan-ability; he was the *Melrose Place*-type actor of his day, and had appeared in feature films like *Palm Springs Weekend* (released in 1969 — with Robert Conrad, no less) — and his last big feature hit was the satirical horror flick, *Love At First Bite* (which was released in 1979). Bottom line? Conrad and Hamilton needed a hit — and *Two Fathers* was their ticket to re-stardom.

Unfortunately, the two actors did not see eye-to-eye. When two stars don't get along, especially when working on the same project, well, one doesn't need a rocket scientist to predict that fireworks will ignite between the performers, and not in a good way. Such was the case with Conrad and Hamilton — at least it appeared that way during the press conference for *Fathers*, during NBC's Press Tour in the fall of 1985 at the Century Plaza Hotel in Century City, California on Century Earth, the Universe.

The Conrad/Hamilton interaction was quite unpleasant, and not very attractive, despite Conrad's bulging biceps or George's gorgeous tan. There they were: James West vs. the dashing Dracula, both of whom were fielding questions from the press about their new NBC-TV movie. But it just wasn't working out, at least not for Conrad.

Remember what I said about bullies? That kind of describes Bobby Conrad. It's as if he was reliving those battery TV commercials that helped pay his mortgage in the in-between years; like he was prodding Hamilton to "Go ahead — knock it off" (the proverbial battery off his shoulder). Whenever a member of the press asked a question, Conrad would reply with a sarcastic tone and yield the query to Hamilton. "Well," Conrad would retort, "maybe George could answer that better than I could." Or, "I don't know, what do you think, George?" Or, "Hey, George, whadda'ya'think, just because you got that tan, you're better than me?"

All of us, including me and my fellow Pages in the room, as well as the members of the press, were aghast at Conrad's behavior. Then again, none of us were going to do anything about it. Hamilton just sat there in silence, shook his head in disbelief, and did not even attempt to defend himself against the bully Conrad. So the rest of us figured, "Why should we?" Also, too, no one wanted to suffer the consequences and/or get their ass kicked with an additional assault and...*battery*.

CHAPTER 18

I Dreamt Of Jeannie: 15 Years Later

Around the same time of the George Hamilton-Robert Conrad debacle, NBC was also promoting a little ditty of a TV-movie entitled, *I Dream of Jeannie: 15 Years Later*. This small-screen film was one of many small-screen films that came to be known as *TV-Reunion Movies* (TRUMS) — after first showing up some years before with *Return to Gilligan's Island* (now, there's a benchmark for you).

During my reign as a Page, TRUMS were sprouting up all over the place, including NBC's own *Return To Mayberry*, which was a re-gathering of the stars, characters and stories of the CBS 1960s classic *The Andy Griffith Show*). With *Jeannie: 15*, NBC brought back the retro central characters from its original 1965-70 hit sitcom, *I Dream Of Jeannie*, which materialized on-screen due to the success of ABC's hit magical sitcom *Bewitched*. In fact, NBC had initially asked *Bewitched* creator Sol Saks to develop another witch show, but he declined. "I had already created one witch show," he had said at the time. "I didn't want to do another." As a result, NBC approached soon-to-be-mini-series king Sidney Sheldon to create *Jeannie*.

Yet I digress — which isn't hard for me to do when talking about *Bewitched*, but nonetheless I digress. So back to *Jeannie: 15*, for which, like *Two Fathers*, I had worked the press tour. Apparently, in the process, I had also ruffled a few feathers of some fellow Pages — and it all had to do with me experiencing more in-person time with *Jeannie* star Barbara Eden than the other GRPs.

My Page supervisor had assigned me as the OIC for this particular sector of the Fall Press Tour of 1985 that was attended by Ms. Eden. I originally perched myself outside the Press Room, while I assigned various members of my Page team on the interior. After the *Father* stars Robert Conrad and George Hamilton were through fighting over who had the bigger, uhm... egos, Barbara had arrived to meet the press.

Remember, now, I had recently already encountered Ms. Eden at the *Hall of Fame Awards*, inadvertently thinking that she was approaching me for a date, when in fact, she simply asked me to guide her to the bathroom. Despite that slight, I remained a fan, and was still very much interested in whatever she had to say about *Jeannie: 15* (especially because too, in the back of my head, I had some secret desire to create and write a TV-reunion movie for *Bewitched*). So, while stationing myself outside the Press Room might have offered me the opportunity for more power ("Hey, you — buddy...get away from that water fountain!), I truly wanted to spend as much time as I could inside, listening to Barbara talk about *Jeannie: 15*. So, I finagled a few things, and made sure I spent more time on the interior, and less time on the exterior. Consequently, and unfortunately, as I said, a few fellow Pages on my team became quite upset with my re-positioning. "Herbie," one of them complained. "What's this about you staying inside so much to listen to Barbara Eden? There are other Pages that are fans of *I Dream of Jeannie*, too, you know. We'd also like to hear her talk about the new movie just as much as you would. So, what's going on?"

"First of all," I should have said (but didn't), "I am the OIC, and I can do pretty much anything what I want. Back-off, Page-Boy!"

Again: let me be clear: I should have said that. But I didn't. Instead, I caved, and allowed the little baby Page-boy to walk into Paradise (the Press Room) and listen to Eden. I eventually caught and heard glimpses here and there of what Eden was saying, as I peeked my head inside from time-to-time. Quite frankly, she really didn't seem like she had a lot to say. There was no spark between her and the press, like there had been during the Hamilton/Conrad interaction. In fact, Eden seemed kind of, well...empty.

As such, I ultimately became more content outside the press room after all, even though it was cold, and that water fountain that everyone seemingly became obsessed with, was turning to ice — though not any more frozen or chilly than the response I received from a few of my fellow Pages during what now became known as the *Jeannie: 15 Debacle*, which also of course alluded to the fact that Wayne Rogers (of *M*A*S*H* fame) had stepped into play *Jeannie's* master-turned-spouse *Major Anthony Nelson* opposite Eden, instead of Larry Hagman who created the role.

But we won't go there.

CHAPTER 19

Page On A Wire

The personal Page relations department (as opposed to the Guest Relations Department of Pages) was a unique beast. You had to dance around certain Pages to get along with them, walk on coals, proceed gingerly, and all those kinds of things. I immediately became observant of this strange interpersonal behavior from the minute I started working at NBC — and continued to experience it when other new Pages were hired in different classes every two months or so. Everyone was just so sensitive.

Actually, everyone in the entertainment industry is sensitive; or ultimately, insecure, which is really a better word to describe us. None of us in show business knows exactly how long any particular gig is going to last, so we all try to hold on to whatever we're doing at the moment as much as possible. Sometimes, we hold on, too tightly. We learn early on just how difficult it is to feel secure in such an insecure business, where personnel replacements are a dime a dozen, and personal emotions are considered immature and unprofessional. One is not allowed to have real emotions. So, go figure. Life was no different for Pages. Not only was everyone sensitive, but everyone just seemed to take things the wrong way. Like Connie Jones, who had recently been promoted to Page Supervisor.

Connie and I got off on the wrong foot from the get-go. It was like I was in love with her or something, because every time I was around her, I flubbed my words and got sweaty. But I knew it wasn't love. I just plain became nervous around her — as when one particular day, our association became even more uncomfortable.

I'm not exactly sure what I said that day, but it all came out the wrong way, and Connie totally misperceived what was stated. I made an attempt at humor, and she thought I was positioning her as the butt of a sarcastic joke, but such was not the case. Shortly after the misinterpretation, I entered Connie's office. She was just sitting there at her desk, with her head down in paper work. I literally stretched out my arm, offered her my hand, and said, "I'm sorry." Connie peered up from her paperwork, and was like, "Uh?" She had not a clue as to what I was doing, and could not have possibly cared less. It also seemed like she failed to even comprehend what was happening. It was like someone had never reached out and apologized to her about anything. There I was trying to do so for no reason except misperception.

Finally, because my arm and hand remained stretched for some time, Connie begrudgingly lifted her right arm, and shook my hand. I then left her office, and for the next few days, our association continued to be slightly chilly. Then, a miracle of sorts transpired: Johnny Carson had decided that he was going to impersonate Willie Nelson while singing the latter's hit single, *To All The Girls I Loved Before* — with Julio Iglesias (who, that particular evening, was making a guest appearance on *The Tonight Show*).

One of the many neat things about the Page lounge is that the television situated inside was linked with NBC's main video feed to all the studios. Not only could you walk in there, plop yourself down and watch anything on TV just like you were in your own home, but Pages in the lounge also had access to things like rehearsals over at *Days of the Our Lives* and the short-lived daytime soap *Sunset Beach* (the latter for which I auditioned).

So, there I was, flippin' TV (feed) channels this one day in the lounge. The rehearsal for the *Tonight Show* pops up, and there's Johnny in full *Willie Nelson* regalia, along with Julio Iglesias, belting out their '80s hit, *To All The Girls I Loved Before*. Don't know why, but I could not stop laughing. I mean, laughing, uncontrollably. It probably had nothing to do with the fact that Carson was a true comic genius, because I wasn't aware of things like that at the time. I just thought it was plain, flat-out hilarious that Johnny was impersonating Willie Nelson with Julio. Or maybe I was just nervous and I needed an emotional outlet? Or maybe, down deep in my subconscious, I wanted Connie to hear me, while she was sitting in her Page supervisor's office, which was only a mere nine feet away from the Page lounge?

Either way, Connie did indeed hear me laughing, so much so, she was once again distracted away from her paperwork. Into the lounge she arrived, looked at me, glanced over at the TV, shook her head, rolled her eyes, smiled a little bit, as if to say, "You *are* a little off, aren't ya'" and returned to her office.

After that, whenever Connie and I saw one another, we were always cordial. The whole mini-bad-blood-thing that was based on God-only-knows-what had dissipated. Connie and I had become friends, and she never made me sweat — in a bad way — ever again.

Thank you, Johnny, Julio and Willie.

CHAPTER 20

The Screaming Room

One of the legitimately big issues that I experienced with my superiors in the NBC Guest Relations Department was ignited when I signed up for the tech assistant position at in the Screening Room.

The SR was located in the main office building of NBC, on the second floor, two stairways up from the infamous NBC commissary about which Johnny Carson often joked. Pages were not only assigned to perform different duties across the board (giving tours, working in the ticket office, etc.), but we also were allowed to sign up or volunteer for certain services. I considered myself more in the creative/performance spectrum of the industry. I wanted to increase my technical knowledge, which I never really gave a second thought, while growing up. But because of the Page position, my interest in behind-the-scenes mechanisms increased. I had directed main stage plays in college, but I had not contemplated the possibilities of directing television shows.

At the time, only a few actors were directing. Robert Redford (who commenced his astounding career with guest appearances on TV shows like CBS' late '50s/early '60s hit, *The Twilight Zone*) had made a name for himself by helming feature films like *Ordinary People* (starring a very un-Laura-Petrie-Mary-Richards Mary Tyler Moore) and *The Natural* (which was shot in Buffalo, New York, just a hop, skip and a jump from my hometown Rochester). NBC's very own Michael Landon certainly made a name for himself as the star and resident director of *Little House on the Prairie* and *Highway to Heaven* (after cutting his teeth a little bit in the last few seasons of *Bonanza* on NBC in the early 1970s). Meanwhile, too, *Heaven* was fast becoming one of NBC's new hit shows and slowly helping to rebuild and restore the network's reputation for breeding hits during the 18 months that I was a

Page. So the time was right to venture full-throttle into the industry's tech world — and the Screening Room seemed like a good place to start.

The SR was run by a curmudgeon of a little man who I'll call Harry, simply because I can't really remember his name. A few of my Page peers had requested extended assignments there with Harry. One Page in particular was Margie Kosaker, a great friend who had been dating another solid Page pal named Stu Barker. Margie and Stu were the ultimate fun couple of the Pages, and I always used to admire their relationship. In fact, I envied it, and I wanted so much for me and Susie Lynn to have what Margie and Stu experienced. But, again, such was not meant to be.

In any case, one day, Margie was assigned to the Screening Room. I was on a break in the Page lounge, and the phone rings. Usually, those closest to the phone were required to answer it. Picking up the receiver many times meant the possibility of being assigned an extra tour for the day, or it could also have meant that your Aunt Tillie had passed away, and that you needed to fly home immediately. For me on this particular day, it meant neither. Instead, when I picked up the phone, Margie was on the other side. "Herbie!" she screamed in my ear, "I'm in the screening room, and we're viewing dailies of *From Between the Darkness and the Dawn*, starring Elizabeth Montgomery... and she's naked! Naked! Get your ass up here ASAP."

Clearly, Margie was more than aware of my *Bewitched* fandom, though how could she or any other Page not have been. Many times you would find me on the floor of the Page lounge, stomach down, feet up in the air, staring in front of the TV, salivating over a rerun of *Bewitched* like I was 12 years old. Suffice it to say, my Samantha-obsession was common knowledge.

Meanwhile, too, please understand that the dailies viewed in the SR were unedited sequences from the television shows and TV-movies that were yet to air. It wasn't as though Elizabeth was filming any kind of actual nude scene that would ultimately make it into the final cut. She was simply filming the scene while nude, and the sequence would be appropriately edited at a later time. That was part of the whole process of screening the dailies in the SR in the first place: to pre-edit.

In any case, not more than 3 minutes after Margie relayed the Montgomery message, I arrived in the SR, but... I was too late. The nude sequences with Elizabeth had ended. I was now only observing a scene where she was reading a book in some library. Needless to say, I was disappointed.

However, it still was fun to see Elizabeth years before I would interview her for my *Bewitched Book*, its subsequent revision, entitled, *Bewitched Forever*, and a new planned biography, *Twitch Upon A Star: The Elizabeth Montgomery Story*. So, I stuck around for a little bit in the SR, and later returned to the Page lounge, where I completed my lunch break. If anything, I was at least now more inspired than ever to register for an assignment in the Screening Room. But that would prove to be a dire move.

The following week, I found myself scheduled for a two-day stay in the SR — and I hated it. In fact, I hated it so much that, after I flubbed working the projector, I left in a huff of frustration. As a result, my supervisors strung me up by the balls. I was called into the office and surrounded by at least five superiors, including Jesse Gomez, who was the supervisor of the supervisors; the *I Remember Mama* look-a-like who reported to Eba Hawkins (the smoking, heavy-drinking Lucille Ball *sound-and-look-a-like*). Jesse also used to fancy himself a comedian. Both he and Tony Pete, in fact, used to walk around the studio doing really bad impersonations of Billy Crystal's really bad impersonation of Fernando Lamas (father to Lorenzo Lamas, who found fame via the 1978 big-screen hit *Grease* and CBS's *Falcon Crest*).

Jesse was also the guy who refused to put my "J" (with or without a period) on my name tag when I was first hired as a page. Apparently, that was too big of a request (and his refusal to do so was partly due to his testing my integrity). At any rate, Jesse and company really let me have it. "Who do you think you are? When a Page requests an assignment, they must stick to the assignment! Do you hear that, Pilato? Stick to it! This isn't Rochester, New York, you know. You just can't waddle in and out of this office and think that we're gonna coddle you!"

"I know, I know. I'm sorry."

"You should be sorry, soldier! You're about two inches away from getting fired."

"But...?"

"But nothing. Now get back to work. You're assigned to only give tours for the next two weeks. Good day, Sir."

"But..."

"I said good day, Sir"

Needless to say, that day was anything but good, and ended badly.

Photos of Pages on Several Pages

I graduated from Nazareth College of Rochester in May 1983, moved into my first Los Angeles and "controversial" apartment in September 1983, and adorned my beige *Mr. Roarke-Fantasy Island-NY-state-of-mind-three-piece suite* on my first day of work as a Page for NBC in May 1984.

The Pritikin Longevity Center, Santa Monica, California

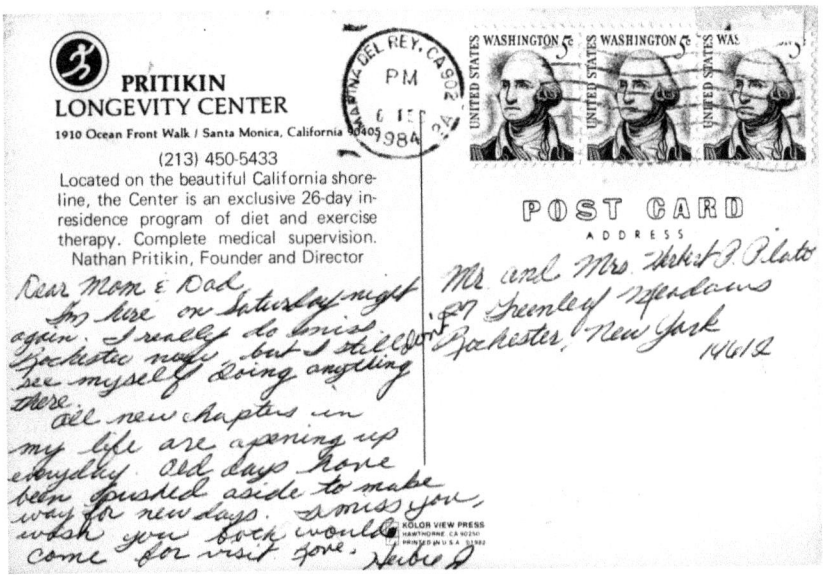

Shortly before I began life as a Page, I worked as a front desk clerk at the Pritikin Longevity Center in Santa Monica. I made a kindly personal visit to a senior resident in their apartment, and I was fired — though not before I had the opportunity to meet NBC's *Star Trek* creator Gene Roddenberry (who frequented the Pritikin). Around this time, I was also constantly writing my parents back in Rochester about the new *chapters* in my life.

```
                                                    Santa Monica, CA   90403
                                                    July 11, 1984

MR. GENE RODDENBERRY

Beverly Hills, CA  90210

Dear Mr. Gene Roddenberry:

First, allow me to re-introduce myself.  I met you at the Pritikin
Longevity Center when I was working at the front desk.  As you were
checking out, I said to myself, "Ok, Herbie.  This is a once in a
lifetime chance to meet Gene Roddenberry."

Although I did get up enough nerve to ask you for an autograph, I was
so thrown by your presence, that I was unable to express all that I
felt.

The following is a brief summary of what I've always wanted to say to
you:

     "Since Star Trek went on the air in 1966, I have been one of the
     millions of fans whose heart has over and over again been warmed
     by your work.

     Whenever I was downhearted, I could always look forward to viewing
     an episode of Star Trek knowing that my spirit would be uplifted."

When you graciously gave me your autograph, you signed it, "Live long
and prosper.  Love, Gene Roddenberry."

While I only worked at the Pritikin for a short time, I know now that
the sole reason for me having that job, was so that I could have the
honor (and fulfill a lifelong dream ) of meeting you.

Destiny was never planned so well.

I consider myself a man who understands what you have succeeded in telling
the world...that there is hope.

Currently I am working as an N.B.C. page and seeking an entry level
position in television and film production.

In advance, thank you for your time and consideration, and I hope to
hear from you in the near future...or at least before stardate 9/1/84.

                                                    Sincerely,

                                                    *Herbert J. Pilato*
                                                    Herbert J. Pilato
```

Approximately four months after I became an NBC Page — and about nine months after I met Gene *Star Trek* Roddenberry at the Pritikin Longevity Center, I (as *Herbert J.* — with period) asked the *Great Bird of the Galaxy* for a job. He turned me down, but with one of the most awesome rejection letters (in which he addressed me as just plain Herbert) I had ever received – on *Enterprise* stationary, no less. *(See illustration on next page).*

August 1, 1984

Herbert J. Pilato
Santa Monica, CA 90403

Dear Herbert:

Thank you for the nice letter and the compliments. I am pleased to see that you have begun working at NBC as a page, as that job often can lead to greater things. Although we do not have any positions open in our staff, I shall certainly keep your resume in our file should anything turn up.

Meanwhile, best of luck in all your future endeavors.

Live long and prosper!

Gene Roddenberry

GR:ss

NBC Memorandum

To: Herby Pilato
From: Pat Griffith
Date: December 19, 1984
Subject: LIMOUSINE RUN NBC TALENT AIRLINE DEPARTURE

DATE OF DEPARTURE: FRIDAY, DECEMBER 21
YOU WILL BE PICKED UP AT: Santa Monica
TIME: 9:30 PM
TO ACCOMPANY: Michael J. Fox
ADDRESS: Paramount Studios, Stage 24
FAMILY TIES-
TALENT PICK UP TIME: 10:00 PM
DEPARTING ON: 12/21 AIRLINE: U.S. Air
FLIGHT #: 602
FLIGHT DESTINATION: Philadelphia
DEPARTURE TIME: 11:45 PM

SPECIAL INSTRUCTIONS:

Town & Country Limousine

If you have any questions or problems, contact Rose Meade at home through the NBC operator or at work at .

Here's the schedule for the limo-run to pick up my short compadre Michael J. Fox. Notice: the memo is address to "Herby" Pilato. I mean, it was bad enough that not everyone addressed me as "Herbie J" (with no period), now Pat Griffith was replacing my "ie" with a "y." "Why" indeed?

A few NBC stars with whom I experienced limo-run-ins — *Top Left: Diff'rent Strokes* dad Conrad Bain (top left). *Top Right: Hill Street Blues* man James B. Sikking. *Bottom Left: Night Court*'s Harry Anderson. *Bottom Right: Knight Rider/Baywatch* lead David Hasselhoff, seen here with Parker Stevenson. (Stevenson is the former husband of NBC *Cheers* star Kirstie Alley who, during her now famous appearance at the 1991 Emmy Awards, thanked her then-spouse for giving her "the big one" during their entire wedded-run.)

Top Left: Family Ties star Michael J. (WITH period). *Top Right:* Fox, me, *Ties* co-star Tina Yothers, and a few fellow Pages at an NBC Press Tour. *Middle Left:* Me and Brooke Shields backstage at The Tonight Show. *Middle Left:* Me with the sweet and beautiful models from *Sale of the Century*. *Bottom Left:* Me with *Miami Vice* star Sandra Santiago. *Bottom Right:* Sandra, solo.

Always and Forever (by Heatwave): That's what I used to sing during many audience warm-up sessions for the various shows that I worked on as a Page – and as I'm doing here for *The New Let's Make A Deal*. In fact, on this particular day, The *Los Angeles Times* visited the Guest Relations Department for a feature article, and they needed an angle for a story. So I gave them one.

I left my initial apartment on South Bundy Drive in West L.A., and moved to another little studio pad, this time, located in Santa Monica at 17th Street and Santa Monica Boulevard (behind the Taco Bell). I lived in Apartment 9. My neighbor in Apartment 8 was actor Louis Herthum *(Top)*, who played *Sheriff Andy* on *Murder, She Wrote*. Meanwhile, Phil Donahue once brought his Philadelphia-based show for a week-long taping at NBC Burbank. He's seen here *(Bottom)* interviewing former-talk-show peer John Davidson (who hosted NBC's *New Hollywood Squares* during my time as a Page).

The Gretchen Page or *Gretchen: The Page*. However you want to word it, Gretchen Harris, was and remains a great friend. During her Page days, she may have been seen conducting tours in NBC's Mini-Studio *(Top Left)*, or with me at various NBC parties *(Top Right)*, or next to her special parking space for NBC's *60th Anniversary Special (Bottom Left)*. Today *(Bottom Right)*, she's lives happily in Sacramento, California with her husband Randy, and their three children: Grace (7), and twins Ian and Megan (4).

Top: That's me with fellow Pages Candy Franklin and Jeff Meschel (who later held various esteemed and subsequent positions as an Assistant, Manager, Director and Vice President of NBC Casting) at an NBC Press Party in the Fall of 1984. (Jeff went on to hold a highly-regarded position in NBC casting.) *Bottom:* Page *Survivors:* In a very rare display of competition (yeah, right) NBC Pages worked with Pages from ABC and CBS at an awards ceremony. Standing next to me is a wonderful NBC Pagette named Kris Keller ("Would you please pour as I drink?" — and only she knows what that means). Next to Kris: a non-NBC Page who looked like Darrin (from *Bewitched*). Two female Pages to my left is a non-NBC pagette who's real name was Tabitha. The real tall guy at in the top row? That's the brother of *Three's Company* star Jenilee Harrison.

Two *wonderful bunches of coconut Pages*, including the now famous Mike Naninni *(Top Photo, far right)*, Roger Hyman *(Bottom Photo, far left)*, Sim Dulaney *(Top Photo, far left; Bottom Photo, top row)*, Linda Stanton *(Top Photo, third from the right; Bottom Photo, second from the left)* and Steve Leon *(Top Photo, fifth from the left; Bottom Photo, far right)*.

My Face On A Page (Six times): *Top Left:* I know it looks like I was a freshman in high school, but this photo was actually taken two years after I became a Page. *Top Right:* A "character" shot (with unibrow yet to be man-scaped) that was photographed in the General Manager's office at the Marriott Airport Hotel in Rochester before I moved to LA in 1983. *Middle Left:* Me and my '70s mullet in the '80s. *Middle Right:* A quaint Page pic, relaxing at one of the many Page parties. *Bottom Left:* My *tough/hot-guy* look. *Bottom Right:* An *author photo* that has made the rounds for years.

Tag—I was it!: It was always important to have the proper identification through my various pre-Page incarnations (as a bellman for the Marriott Airport Hotel in Greece, New York; as a student of Theatre at Nazareth College of Rochester), and during my actual life as a Page. However, my superiors in each case always had an issue with correctly labeling my name tags or ID cards minus the period after my "J". In fact, I got everything but — except for the time when, as a joke, the maintenance supervisor at the Marriott created a mock-up tag that actually read "HERBIE J (NO PERIOD)." That was pretty funny.

HOORAY FOR HOLLYWOOD - HERB!

Herbie J. Pilato, former P.M. Van Driver, who moved to Los Angeles after graduating from Nazareth College, has landed a bit part in a new movie, **Hadley's Rebellion**, starring Griffen O'Neal (Ryan's son), Charles Durning, and William DeVane!! Atta way to go Herbie J.!

He's also taking drama courses at U.C.L.A. and working at a seaside Hotel in Santa Monica. He says, "he is having the time of his life." We'll be watching the Academy awards, in April, with our fingers crossed.

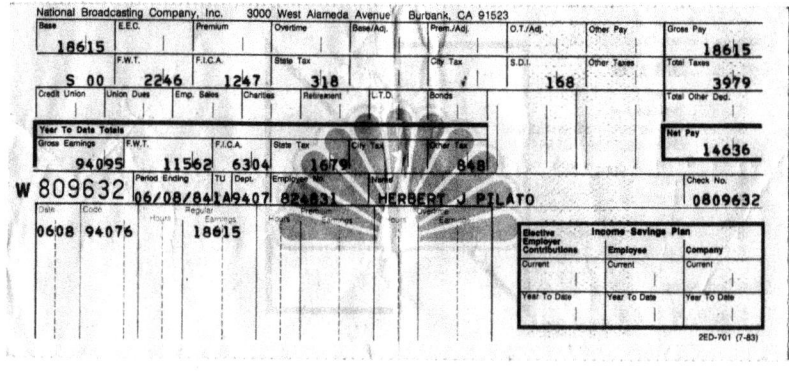

Oh, the dichotomy: Top: A news clip from the Marriott Airport Hotel Newsletter (titled, *The Mariodyssey)*, which made mention of my move to LA (and my acting potential). *Bottom:* A reality check in the form of a weekly paystub from my modest Page salary.

NBC Monthly Show Taping Schedule
3000 West Alameda Avenue, Burbank, California 91523

SEPTEMBER 1984

Sunday	Monday	Tuesday	Wednesday	Thursday	Friday	Saturday
						1 SBL 12:00 N SBL 2:30 PM LMD 3:00 PM LMD 7:30 PM
2	3	4 WOF 3:00 PM TNT 5:30 PM WOF 6:30 PM	5 WOF 4:00 PM TNT 5:30 PM WOF 7:00 PM FJ TBA	6 TNT 5:30 PM FB 8:00 PM	7 SOC 2:00 PM TNT 3:00 PM SOC 4:45 PM TNT 5:30 PM WOF 6:30 PM	8 WOF 4:00 PM SOC 5:00 PM WOF 7:00 PM SOC 7:45 PM
9	10 WOF 3:00 PM TNT 5:30 PM WOF 6:30 PM	11 TNT 5:30 PM	12 TNT 5:30 PM	13 TNT 5:30 PM FB 8:00 PM	14 PB 12:30 PM TNT 5:30 PM	15 PB 12:30 PM
16	17	18 SOC 2:00 PM SOC 4:45 PM TNT 5:30 PM	19 SOC 5:00 PM TNT 5:30 PM SOC 7:45 PM SP TBA	20 TNT 5:30 PM FB 8:00 PM SP TBA	21 PB 12:30 PM WOF 3:00 PM TNT 5:30 PM WOF 6:30 PM	22 WOF 4:00 PM WOF 7:00 PM
23 SBL 1:30 PM SBL 4:15 PM	24 SBL 12:00 N SBL 2:30 PM WOF 3:00 PM WOF 6:30 PM	25 SBL 12:00 N SBL 2:30 PM TNT 5:30 PM	26 TNT 5:30 PM	27 TNT 5:30 PM SP TBA SP TBA	28 PB 12:30 PM TNT 5:30 PM SP TBA SP TBA	29
30						

FB "FIGHT BACK!"
FJ "FUNNIEST JOKE"
LMD "LET'S MAKE A DEAL"
PB "PUNKY BREWSTER"
SBL "SCRABBLE"
SOC "SALE OF THE CENTURY"
SP "SUPER PASSWORD"
TNT "THE TONIGHT SHOW"
WOF "WHEEL OF FORTUNE"

1. All shows are subject to change without notice.
2. Ticket holders should arrive at the Studio no less than one hour before show time. Please check ticket for minimum age limit.
3. NBC TOURS. Go behind the scenes of television. Continuous tours from 9:00 AM to 5:00 PM daily. Tickets may be purchased at Studio or at all California Ticketron outlets. Closed Thanksgiving, Christmas and New Year's Day.
4. NBC Merchandise Counter open from 9 AM to 5 PM daily.
Please read reverse side.

A typical NBC schedule that Pages referenced, while answering questions from the general public (on the phone or in person) in the Ticket Office and Ticket Booth.

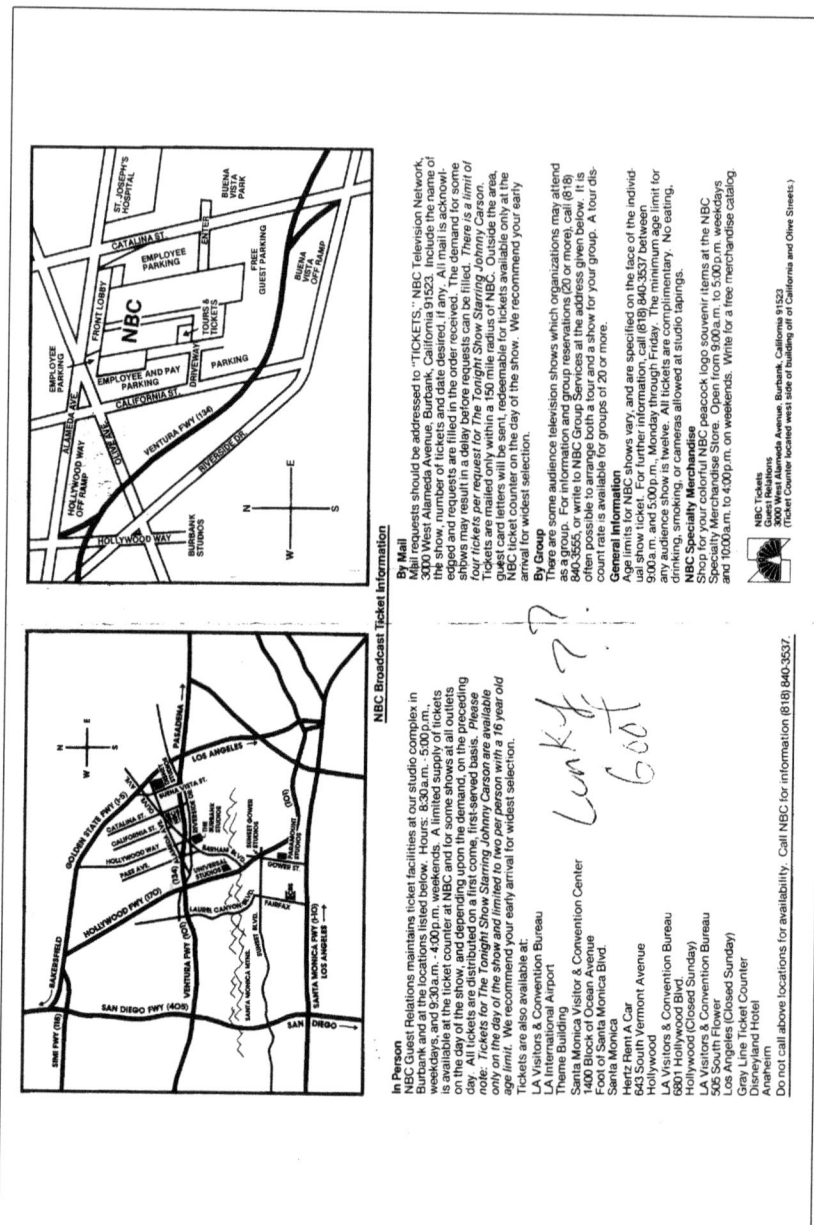

The flip-side of the NBC Schedule referenced by the Pages in the Ticket office and Ticket Booth. This particular copy has scribbled upon it the words, *Lunky Goof,* which marked the day that I conversed on the phone with someone who was having a challenging time understanding the title of the show I was referencing *(Punky Brewster).*

NBC   National Broadcasting Company, Inc.   3000 West Alameda Avenue
Burbank, CA 91523

December 10, 1982

Mr. Herbert Pilato
Santa Monica, Ca

Dear Mr. Pilato:

Thank you for your interest in pursuing employment opportunities with the National Broadcasting Company.

After a careful review of your qualifications we find that we do not have a position for you at the present time. However, in light of your experience, we are taking the liberty of retaining your resume in our active file for future reference and will call you if an appropriate position becomes available.

We appreciated the opportunity to review your application and wish you success in your future career endeavors.

Sincerely,

Jean Ford
Jean Ford
Employment Coordinator

It took persistence to attain my job as an NBC Page, and persistence is what I had, even following rejection after rejection *(which see next illustration)* from the network. Notice, too, how "Dear Mr. Pilato" has been inserted into what clearly is a form letter — making the rejection, of course, all the more impersonal and insincere.

National Broadcasting Company, Inc.
3000 W. Alameda Ave.
Burbank, Ca 91523

Thank you for your recent resume/application for employment with the National Broadcasting Company.

We regret that we do not have a position for you at the present time but, after a review of your qualifications, would like to keep your application in our active file for future reference. We will call you if an appropriate position becomes available.

We wish you success in your future career endeavors.

Sincerely,

Greg Holden
Staffing Specialist

American Broadcasting Company 4151 Prospect Avenue Hollywood, California 90027 Telephone

September 2, 1982

Mr. Herbert Pilato
Santa Monica, Ca 90403

Dear Mr. Pilato:

Thank you for submitting information concerning your experience and skills for our consideration.

We have carefully evaluated your qualifications relative to the requirements of our current openings. Although your skills and experience are excellent we regret that a suitable position is not available at this time. However, your application will be retained, reviewed over the next few months and should a position occur, you will be contacted.

We appreciate your interest in working for the American Broadcasting Companies, Inc. and wish you every success in finding the opportunity you are seeking.

Sincerely,

Dean Feruce
Staffing Representative

DF/cy

Even after rival network ABC rejected me (with this letter), I tried once more with NBC. Finally, by the grace of NBC Page Horris Smith, I won an interview with Eba Hawkins.

AL LOWE ASSOCIATES, INC.
5815 East Parkside Drive
Fresno, California 93727

209 255-8551

December 3, 1984

Ms. Eba Hawkins
NBC Guest Relations
3000 W. Alameda Avenue
Burbank, CA 91523

Dear Ms. Hawkins

I wish to express my appreciation for the service and kindness shown me by one of your employees, HERBIE J. PILATO. He was directly responsible for averting a "family disaster" last Saturday by reacting with service "above and beyond" the call of normal duties.

To explain: my husband was scheduled to be a contestant on "Name That Tune's" Saturday taping. My 8-year old son and I drove five hours to LA, but went to the wrong studio. They directed us to another studio, which directed us to yet another studio (this repeated in total, 5 times!). Each information desk person would merely say, "sorry, we don't tape that," and hand me a map to another studio.

By the time we arrived at NBC we were 5 minutes late, lost, and frustrated. Fortunately, you employed someone who cared enough to listen and offer to help, instead of brushing us off. Herbie and George must have spent 10 minutes making phone calls, but they finally found out I needed to be at KTLA (which was one block from the first studio I tried). They even made a detailed map, with freeway instructions for me!

If they had just "done their job" like the others, I know we would have never found the right place, and our entire trip would have been for nothing. Instead, we made it in time to give my husband the clean shirt he needed, and got to watch him win his show!!

Please express our appreciation to Herbie for his courtesy and helpfulness, and assure him he was solely responsible for turning a family disaster into a marvelous family experience!

Sincerely yours

Margaret Lowe
Vice-president

PS The only network shows we watch are Cheers, Hill St., and Carson (but that may just be coincidental)!!

Excellent!
Eba

Once NBC finally hired me as a Page, the accolades commenced, if after an initial bumpy ride.

NBC Memorandum

To: File of Herbie J. Pilato
From: Supervisors, Guest Relations
Date: Jan. 8, 1985
Subject: Performance

Last Saturday, Jan. 5, a group of children from the Braile Institute showed up unexpectedly. Herbie did an exceptional job with them. We feel his extra effort is to be commended. He spent extra time on his tour, and did his best to ensure they enjoyed themselves. Bravo Herbie.

George Barrett

A truly special letter of accommodation that I received from one of the great (and more sincere) Page supervisors of all time: George Barrett.

hanna barbera land

August 6, 1985

General Manager
NBC Television Studio Tour
3000 W. Alameda Avenue
Burbank, CA 91523

Dear General Manager:

I would like to thank you and your staff for providing a truly enjoyable and informative tour of your studios. We would particularly like to commend our tour guide, Herbie, and unfortunately we did not get his last name. We were in tour number 10 last Tuesday, July 30, at 12:00 noon. His enthusiasm and personality was contagious and everyone in our group had a wonderful time.

We were very impressed with your entire staff. Thanks for a superb tour.

Sincerely,

Eleanor Egan

Eleanor Egan
Marketing Representative
HANNA BARBERA LAND - HOUSTON

See - There's a little compliment every once in awhile - Thanks for a good job!
Eba

A note from from a happy tour attendee, who wrote to Eba Hawkins (the Head of NBC Guest Relations, and Lucille Ball look-and-sound-a-like) — on my behalf

NBC Enterprises

A Division of
National Broadcasting Company, Inc.

3000 West Alameda Avenue
Burbank, CA 91523

Eba Hawkins
Director, Guest Relations
West Coast

January 22, 1986

To Whom It May Concern:

In the time that Herbie J. Pilato worked for the NBC Guest Relations Department (5/84-12/85), he was an extremely responsible, creative, and good public relations representative.

Herbie J. displayed initiative, imagination, problem solving capabilities, and an aptitude for organization even in high pressure situations. He was chosen for special assignments as well. One of Herbie J.'s greatest talents was his ability to deal with all kinds of people in a wide variety of circumstances.

Although Herbie J. is capable of working independently, he is also a team player. His knowledge of the entertainment industry is an asset.

Sincerely,

Eba Hawkins
Director, Guest Relations

EH/kap

I left NBC — and Eba Hawkins — with my "period" and yet also high praise.

CHAPTER 21

A Page In The L.A. Times

A few days after the screening room incident, *The Los Angeles Times* arrived at NBC to do an article on Pages. Many of my peers and supervisors, including a few that yelled at me a mere 48-hours before, offered negative quotes and perspectives on the job. I was also interviewed for the article. As will be detailed in the next chapter, part of the job as a Page was warming up the audiences for game shows like *Wheel of Fortune*, *The New Let's Make A Deal*, *Sale of the Century*, *Scrabble* and *Super Password*.

As fate would have it, on the particular day that the *Times* reporter was interviewing Pages, I happened to be singing to the audience of *The New Let's Make A Deal*. My first number was an a cappella rendition of *Always and Forever*, the big disco hit from the 1970s, made popular by Heatwave. I thought the eyes of the *Times* reporter were going to leap from their sockets, as his note-taking increased to a feverish pace. When I began to belt out, *A Little Lovin'* by Neil Sedaka, well then, forget it. The reporter just lost it. In order to get a better view of the festivities, he climbed on one of the studio seat cushions reserved for the audience, and ordered his photographer to secure a few more shots.

That weekend of September 4, 1985, the Calendar section of the *Times* ran a story on Pages. Placed alongside the article was a massive photo of myself, with a big-ass smile. I was entertaining the troops, all of whom were just as happy to hear me as I was happy to be heard. What's more, my commentary in the article proved to be the sole positive voice of the piece. Consequently, no Page supervisor or anyone else at NBC ever bothered me again.

CHAPTER 22

Super Passwords

Back in the early 1970s, I attended St. Peter and Paul's Catholic Elementary school. We parochial pupils were privileged enough to go home for lunch, mostly because in those days, school was around the corner from where you lived. Also, St. Pete's was a private hall of academia, and students were not bussed all over the place by the Public School system. Every day at 11:30 AM outside St. Pete's on Brown Street, my father would be waiting in his dark green 1969 two-door Pontiac Catalina to pick me up and take me home for my daily dose of hamburgers and Lipton Noodles soup. The daily routine also involved watching then-recent reruns of network shows like CBS' *The Dick Van Dyke Show*, *That Girl* and *Bewitched*, the latter two of which initially aired on ABC.

Somewhere around 1971, the Alphabet network also brought back the classic game show, *Password*, with host Allen Ludden, the one true love of future CBS/*Mary Tyler Moore Show* and NBC/*Golden Girls* star Betty White. Many times, too, my favorite *Bewitched* star Elizabeth Montgomery, who was pretty much too shy to do anything so public and certainly as audience/contestant interactive as a game show, appeared on *Password*. Consequently, *Password*, due mostly to Elizabeth's involvement, along with the frequent appearances of her good friend Carol Burnett, became part of my daytime TV ritual (along with *Match Game '73*, hosted by Gene Rayburn — and also sometimes featuring Betty White).

Who would have thought that some 15 or so years later, I would actually be working as a Page on all my favorite game shows, including an updated version of *Password*, entitled, *Super Password*?

By the time I started ushering in the audience members for *SP*, Allen Ludden had long passed away. Bert Convy, who had partnered with Burt

Reynolds on another popular game show called *Win, Lose or Draw* (which was kinda' sorta like *Pictionary*) had become *SP*'s host. There I was watching, in person, the likes of White and the iconic Lucille Ball playing my favorite TV game show. Such astounding moments towered over the hours I was assigned to work *Wheel of Fortune*, *Scrabble*, *Sale of the Century*, and the then-new edition of *Hollywood Squares* (hosted by former talk show prince John Davidson, replacing icon Peter Marshall). Surely, during this gig at *SP*, I would so hope that Elizabeth would be the guest star on the segments I was assigned to work. She periodically appeared on the show from 1971 to 1979, and now it was 1985 — a mere six years later. I was pining to hear her say that renowned little word — *Pass*. I would have even settled to view any one of her famous facial emotions, which was one of the main reasons she was so much fun to watch in the first place. Seeing funny faces was one of the main reasons why *all* of the original *Password* and *SP* stars were so much fun to watch. Yet, alas, once more, my initial encounter with Elizabeth was not yet meant to be. I would have to wait some four years (until the spring of 1989) to meet (and interview) her.

That said, I would have to "settle" for watching White joke with Ball. The two TV legends were friends, and Ball was a huge fan of White's *Golden Girls*. *Girls* would become the main reason that Ball would consider and then actually return to sitcom TV in 1988, if only with a failed attempt at the genre with the ABC/Aaron Spelling production of *Life With Lucy*.

Had ABC given *Life* a chance and room to breathe, instead of canceling it after only a few episodes, Ball would have had another small screen hit on her hands. Instead, ABC gave up on the show, and did not allow it to find its voice. And that was a real shame, too, because Ball's long-time co-star Gale Gordon, was also cast into *Life*. None of that, however, would transpire until three years after I left NBC.

In the meantime, I would see Lucy once more after *SuperPassword*. This time, it was behind the scenes of *The Tonight Show*, some ten years after her third sitcom, *Here's Lucy*, ended its run CBS, and some four years before her final series, *Life With Lucy*, fizzled on ABC. Sitcom or no sitcom, Ball was a legend. Even though she was also making meager game show appearances, and even though she had not enjoyed sitcom success for nearly ten years (and would never again enjoy it), she was still Lucille Ball from *I Love Lucy*. Her voice was raspy, her gait was manly, and her stance was tall — again, just like Guest Relations manager Eba Hawkins. But standing next to her, with her gaudy red-hair wig, and overly-made-up face, one couldn't help but bow to the awesomeness of who stood before us.

Ball was not only responsible (along with then-husband Desi Arnaz, Jr. and CBS executive Harry Ackerman) for revolutionizing the technique with which television sitcoms were recorded (on tape with a three-camera style in front of a live audience), but she was an on-screen comedic talent that to this day remains unmatched.

It was humbling to see her appear on *SuperPassword*, and it was great see her backstage with Johnny Carson. But I did not fully appreciate her presence until my good friend Mike Nannini ever-so simply reminded me of her astounding talent and presence. In fact, I was all ho-hum about the situation. But Mike set me straight.

"Herbie," he said with a kind, yet firm tone. "This is...*Lucy!*"

Then I got it. I really got it. From that moment on, I was shocked back into awe of Lucille Ball who, at least at two different increments, was not more than twenty feet in front of me.

But as I have pointed out (relentlessly), each time I saw Lucy I couldn't help but visualize NBC Guest Relations boss Eba Hawkins. Just like when I first met Eba all I could think of was Ball. Again, both women were high in stature (physically and career-wise), and had rough, chain-smoking, controlling voices and personalities — at least in their later years. It was particularly jarring to view Ball this way, close-up. That is to say, Eba was a real person; she was allowed to have flaws. But not Ball. She was on a pedestal. She was unreal. And what the heck was a classic TV icon doing on a game show anyway? Lucy was one of the wealthiest people in the industry. Unlike Elizabeth Montgomery, Lucy's appearances on *Password*, were not an emotional outlet and/or rare form of general public interaction. So, I never really understood any of that.

Then again, now that I think about it, maybe Lucy and Eba were friends? Maybe like attracted like? Maybe Eba called Lucy up one day and said, "Lucille...I need you. NBC is putting together this *Super* new edition of *Password*. It's gonna be hosted by Bert Convy. He's a nice guy, but he's no Allen Ludden. So we need big names to guest on the show. We can't wait for Elizabeth Montgomery to call in. She's doing a few TV-movies for us, but not so sure she'd be open to playing *Super Password* — especially without Allen. They got along real fine the first time around. And she might not like Convy. So, whatta'ya say Lucy? Will ya' do the show?"

"Well," Lucy may have replied, "can Gale come on with me?"

"Gale?! You mean Gale *Gordon*?! He's still alive?"

"Yes, Eba. He's still alive..."

"Okay, okay. Gale can come on too."

"Good. And I'll also call Betty White."

"You may be treading on thin ice there, Lucy."

"How do you mean?"

"Betty was married to Allen Ludden, and she may resent Bert Convy."

"Tough. She'll get over it."
"Ah, Lucy…You're my kind of gal."
Now, I guess all they needed to do was contact Bea Arthur.
But that never happened — at least not during my life as a Page.

CHAPTER 23

Is It Door Number 1 or Door Number 2?

Of all the game shows that I worked on at NBC, none was more fun than *The New Let's Make A Deal*.

Like *Super Password*, working on *Deal* was a surreal experience. I had been a fan of the original *Deal* starring Monty Hall and, as with *Password*, I have many fond memories of watching the show as a kid. Whereas I would view *Password* during my lunch hour at home from school at St. Pete's, I got to know *Deal* only on days-off from school, and in the summer (as it was broadcast on ABC at 1:30 in the afternoon).

What struck me most about *Deal* was Monty's main girl, Carol Merrill, who very much resembled Miss Charlene — my third grade teacher at St. Pete's. I could have swore that they were the same person, but with a split personality. Like Wonder Woman and Diana Prince — only they were both really Wonder Woman, if you know what I mean? Miss Charlene was so beautiful. Come winter, she adorned this big fur coat, which was similar to the furs Ms. Merrill would model as prizes on *Deal*. Certainly, this coat correlation directly contributed to my Carol/Charlene confusion. Forget, of course, that I had a massive crush on Miss Charlene — an infatuation that was clearly evident one very challenging day in third grade, during an awkward encounter with a female schoolmate.

My fellow third grader's name was Brenda Johnson. And this one fateful day following lunch, she decided to walk through the aisles in our classroom, lifting her knees high with each gaited leg. I knew some kind of trouble was brewing. I saw the proverbial sign-post up ahead — and it's didn't say "stop." It said, "Watch out! That crazy little bitch is gonna hit ya' in the balls!" Sure enough, within seconds, my spider senses weren't the only things that were tingling — as Brenda bopped me right smack-dab in the testicles. I keeled over in wrenching pain, and started bawling my eyes out. Miss Charlene, meanwhile, was there was to see it all, and was so concerned. "Are you okay, Herbie?" she asked (minus the "J", which was, at the time, only employed for use of home, family and friends).

"It hurts! It hurts!" I cried.

"Aw, honey…but where does it hurt?" she said with her massive circular earrings dangling on either side of her perfect face. I hesitated. My mouth, along with my third grade balls, was now numb — and mum was the word. "I can't tell you," I continued to cry. "I can't tell you where."

"What do you mean?" She kept asking, though I think she got it.

Talk about your ball bustin'!

Needless to say, my pre-pubescent equipment was damaged — and the apple of my eye, Miss Charlene — the teacher to whom I had delivered many an apple — wanted to survey the damaged goods. Man, did I just want to bop Brenda back in the balls, if she had any, which, who knows, maybe she did. It took me some sixteen years, but I would ultimately rectify that memory back to the future of *The New Let's Make A Deal* in 1984. If everyone in my real life had somehow reminded me of everyone in my fantasy TV life, and if those two worlds now continued to collide with game show gigs like *Super Password* and *The New Let's Make A Deal*, then maybe — just maybe Carol Merrill -and her Miss Charlene ways, would reach out to me on the set? To be honest, I was getting excited down there, in the same place that Brenda Johnson launched her attack.

Maybe Carol Merrill could take over where Miss Charlene left off? The possibilities were endless.

As such, on my first assignment with *Deal*, I went right up to one of the production assistants and asked about Carol Merrill. "Will she be working on the new show? Would she be there? Would my 'Miss Charlene of the TV world' be on the set?"

Sadly, the answer was no. Truth be told, by the fall of 1984, a good ten years after ABC cancelled the original *Deal*, Ms. Merrill had retired. At least Monty Hall was available, though he was no Carol Merrill, and certainly not even Miss Charlene. He was indeed a good guy, and I did get along with him quite well. But, of course, I certainly wasn't willing to show Monty *my full Monty*, despite the fact that I was excited to do so with Miss Charlene.

Er — I mean…Carol Merrill.

CHAPTER 24

My Own Personal Carmen Miranda

Overall, *The New Let's Make A Deal* proved to be a wonderful experience for me. Not only did I get to meet and befriend more TV idols like Monty Hall, but my time with *Deal* allowed me the chance to be profiled by the *Los Angeles Times*. I was even offered a job as a prize coordinator for the show. But most of all, I loved working *Deal* because I got to meet girls.

One particular day, while working the lines of *Deal*, I observed a fine figure of a young woman adorned with a unique outfit amidst the sea of unusual girly-get-ups. She was an incredibly hot-looking chick, dressed in a kind of powder-blue bikini/skirt with a semi-basket of fruit on her head. To top it all off, this beautiful vision was stacked like Pam Anderson and flashed violet-blue Elizabeth Taylor's eyes — a window to the soul that seemed to zero-in on me as I breezed by the audience line (and delivered my "no cameras/no shouting out" speech). Of course, I couldn't help myself. I'm a Libra. I'm a natural-born flirt. So I was compelled to walk right up to this latter-day Carmen Miranda and say, "Well, aren't you beautiful!" and we went from there. She introduced herself, and gave me her number. As it turned out, she lived way the hell out in Hemet, California, which is somewhere near Palm Springs.

Remember, I was a Page (like you could forget that by now), and I was only making $5.20 an hour. So, driving anywhere to do anything, much less having the kind of money required to spend on a beautiful woman like Carmen was always a challenge. But I paid little mind to my little pay when my big eyes met her. I didn't think twice about how much money I did or did not make — or even if that mattered to her — because she didn't seem to care one way or the other. There was an instant attraction between us, which only went on to prove that when there's chemistry between two people — when there's a legitimate link betwixt a pair of individuals — money, status and financial security does not even play into the game. For Pete's sake, I was dressed in a three-piece pin-striped suit that I adorned every day above worn-out black shoes that were nearly sole-less. The least I could do was have a soul of my own, and not let money make a difference.

So, I drove to Hemet to see Carmen. She was only about 19 years old and, if I recall, she lived with her parents in this awesome, sprawling stucco-styled mansion — the kind that I used to see in Scottsdale, Arizona when I would visit my relatives in Phoenix (and a contemporary-version stucco of the home belonging to David Hasselhoff's married-managers). Come to find out, Carmen wanted to be an actress, and I had every bit of faith that she would reach her goal. She would become a star that would light up the Hollywood skies around the world. Clearly, she had already illuminated my life.

Bottom line: Carmen and I went out a few times, but because she lived so far, it was indeed a challenge to continue seeing her — and not because of the economics of it, but because of the time and effort it required in traveling out to Hemet. Then again, there was also the fact that I was still carrying such a strong torch for Susie Lynn. Yet, though my attraction to Susie Lynn was strong, I knew in my heart of hearts that it was going nowhere. I may have, in fact, used her as a crutch for not moving on with any other relationship, for whatever reason.

At any rate, I would soon have to part with Carmen, my own personal little *Chiquita Banana* girl of Hemet, California. Initially driving from Santa Monica to see her was exciting. But on the way back home, there proved to be some issues.

Evidently, there was something wrong with the muffler on my white Regal. It didn't sound right. Actually, it sounded like it was going to fall off. What made matters worse is that, once on the road, monsoon-like rain began to downpour and seemingly attack only my car. The freeway was drenched with water. I couldn't see two feet in front of me, let alone if there were any other cars on the road. My muffler slid with super-speed on the wet granite highway. With periodic sparks underneath the challenged-vehicle along the way, I could do nothing else but pray. And so I began:

"Our Father, who art in Heaven, hallowed by Thy name..." I went on to repeat the Lord's Prayer, which I had learned and known for years as a good Catholic school boy at St. Pete's. I prayed and prayed and prayed, for miles and miles and miles, all the way from Hemet to Santa Monica — at the very least a 200-mile stretch — through a rapid rainstorm.

Soon my prayers would partially be answered; a miracle would transpire.

The rain stopped, approximately 30 miles outside Santa Monica. The downpour ended, but the uproar of challenges continued. I was soon flagged down by a police car driven by an officer who had clocked me going 75mph for the last 60 minutes. He might have been willing to give me the benefit of the doubt had I trailed off to an even 55mph, but I did not. I went the distance at 75mph for the remaining 55 minutes. I tried to explain to the officer about the muffler, and that I was speeding for safety reasons; that my car was going to explode if I didn't make it home to Santa Monica in time. Though sympathetic to my story, the officer still gave me a ticket. Maybe I should have told him the entire truth; that I was traveling from Hemet, because I met a hot Carmen Miranda look-a-like who was standing in line at *The New Let's Make A Deal*, for which I was Paging in a three-piece pin-striped suit that mini-towered over near sole-less shoes? That just wouldn't have been believable.

Instead, I just kept my mouth shut, as the officer wrote that ticket and recommended that I get myself to a mechanic as soon as I arrived in Santa Monica. I took the ticket in my hand, politely smiled, thanked the kindly policeman, and eventually found my way to a Midas Muffler station. Once the Midas mechanic looked under my car, he was stunned, especially after I told him that I had just driven from Hemet, California. "Somebody must have been looking after you?" he said incredulously. "Boy, you just plain lucky you're alive."

Though I agreed with the mechanic's observations, lady luck would have been more on my side if that policeman didn't give me that ticket — and certainly I would have been luckier if Carmen had lived in Santa Monica instead of Hemet. Still, I wasn't about to debate my good fortune, especially because I did indeed drive back to Hemet to see Carmen a few more times.

Then, of course, too, there was the time Carmen drove all the way to Burbank to see me. Well, sort of. One day, I set out to hand-deliver my actor's photo and resume to an agency on Alameda Avenue that was close by NBC. As I walked down the avenue, I heard this voice, from the other side of the road, screaming from a passing car: "Herbie! Herbie!" I turned my head and there was Carmen — minus the full Miranda outfit, but still flashing those Elizabeth Taylor eyes directly on me. Naturally, I was happy to see her, and yelled back, "Hey!" She then spun her car around from the other side of the street, drove up right next to me on the sidewalk, and we talked a little bit. But after a few minutes, I had to get back to my agency trek, and she had to get back to wherever it was that she was really driving. Though she did insist that I keep in touch.

Unfortunately, I never did. I'm not sure why, really. Maybe it was because of Susie Lynn? Maybe it was because I felt I wasn't good enough for Carmen?

These were questions I continued to ask myself. But Carmen herself never said a word, and she never seemed to care one way or the other if I was a Page or the king of all media. She liked me, and that was that.

I tell you right now: if my little Carmen Miranda look-a-like, originally from Hemet, California, is still available — all these years later — and if those Elizabeth Taylor eyes somehow find their way onto the pages of this book, and onto one particular Page named Herbie J, she should call me right away... so that maybe I can rewrite this chapter — with a happier ending.

CHAPTER 25

The Australian British Aisles

Though uniquely awesome was my sweet Carmen, she was merely one of several young women I encountered as a Page, specifically via *The New Let's Make A Deal*. For example, one very steamy day in Burbank, this very hot — and I do mean hot — blonde showed up in line, dressed as God only knows what... all I know is that she was, again, hot. I mean, sultry, voluptuous super-hot. I think she also had some kind of British/Australian accent thing going on, which only made her hotter. Hmm, did I mention that she was hot?

In either case, I noticed her immediately, and struck up a conversation. Her name was Tippie, and she seemed to like me a great deal. But after what seemed like only a few micro-seconds, the audience was called inside the studio for the show's taping. I was upset because I didn't have a chance to fetch Tippies' number, and my chances for getting together with her were slimming — rapidly.

Once inside the studio myself, I observed *Deal's* resident warm-up comedian working the audience before the show commenced. So off I went in search of a little piece of Heaven on Earth. After only a few seconds, I spotted Tippie, which was not a difficult thing to do. Suffice it to say, Tippie stood out way atop the left-hand side of the studio. Along with the rest of the audience, she was squealing in excitement as the warm-up semi-good-humored man proceeded with the telling of his over-told jokes. I immediately ran up the ump-teen steps to meet up with her and yelled, "I didn't get your number!"

"What?!" she answered back.

"Your number!" I reiterated. "I want your number!!"

Tippie just kind of looked at me, as if stunned that I just ran up what was about two flights of stairs with manic speed simply for this request, and said with her lovely full British/Australian lips, "You've got guts!" She then proceeded to give me her number. The show completed taping, and I called her a few days later. (That's the rule, right? Not to call them the next day?)

Tippie and I ended up spending one beautiful night together, probably one of the best nights of my life — and she went back to what I finally confirmed to be Australia. Thank you, mate. And once again, thank you Monty Hall.

Tippie was one of the best deals I could have sealed while working on your show.

CHAPTER 26

The Ticket Orifice

As mentioned elsewhere in this book, the Ticket Office, particularly — the Ticket Booth (which we Pages termed as the hell hole) was not anywhere near a popular assignment for any Guest Relations Representative. In fact, we all hated that part of the job, mostly because it consisted of eight-hour shifts answering phones (and the same questions, over and over), reading ticket request letters from those who wrote in, and stuffing and addressing hundreds and hundreds of envelopes. At least in the Ticket Office there was interaction with other Pages. But in the Ticket Booth? Forget about it. Just sitting there, for the entire eight-hour shift, was indeed pure hell. When either shift commenced, either in the Office or the Booth, the disposition of assigned Page would be more or less cheery. But by around the end of the second-hour — watch out. No potential audience member better have inquired if there were anymore tickets available for *The Tonight Show* — or any other show — for there would indeed be hell to pay.

Again, at least in the Ticket Office, the selected Page did not have to show his or her face, as most of his or her work with the public was conducted over the phone. People would call up from all over the country and ask for tickets. Each Page would have a show schedule placed in front of them. Most of the accessible shows for potential NBC Burbank audiences were games shows like *Wheel of Fortune, Scrabble, The New Let's Make a Deal, The New Hollywood Squares, Super Password*, and *Sale of the Century*. Everyone, of course, wanted tickets for *The Tonight Show* — but these were the most difficult to attain (even for the VIP seats that were further code-named, Tape-And-Hold). But still, for a fortunate and dedicated few, it happened: they actually attained *Tonight* tickets to see Carson. Many ticket callers would have to plan months and months ahead — sometimes even years — to see the show. But Johnny was the King of Late Night TV, and they were willing to wait.

To my surprise, one day when I was assigned to the office, a woman called in and specifically asked for any other shows besides *Tonight*. I glanced at the list before me, named off a few available shows, including *Punky Brewster*, starring the then-pubescent Soleil Moon Frye (who was little sister to the also then-young actor Meeno Peluce, who co-starred on NBC's short-lived sci-fi/time-travel show *Voyagers!* with the late Jon-Erik Hexum — who would accidentally and very tragically later shoot himself — with a gun loaded with blanks — on the set of the CBS adventure series, *Cover Up*).

In any case, back in the Ticket Office, the woman on the other end of the phone did not understand me when I mentioned the title of Soleil's show, *Punky Brewster*, and replied, *Lunky Goof?!* Upon hearing this woman's interpretation of the show's title, I laughed so hard I had to put her on hold. I found it hilarious not merely because she completely mispronounced the show's title, but because the way she mispronounced it harkened back to an incident surrounding my sister Pam's wedding in 1983, back home in Rochester. My brother-in-law Sam had used the same voice inflection, tone and number of syllables during a conversation we had with regards to a wedding gift that he and my sister Pam (yes their names are Pam and Sam in real life) had received from an elderly couple.

Pam and Sam did not immediately go on their honeymoon, and the day after the wedding, instead went over their gifts and counted their money. There were the regular gifts of can openers, toasters, and such — and the odd ones, like the musical tea server (hat played *Tea for Two*). The average gift for a wedding these days, I believe is somewhere around $50.00. In the '80s, it was at least $25.00 — and maybe you could have slid by with $15.00. But the senior duo had sent my sister and brother-in-law only $5.00, to which Sam responded by adamantly stating, "Five dollars!" in the same exact manner that woman on the phone responded with "*Lunky Goof.*" So, if anyone decides to one day create a show titled *Lunky Goof*, I expect to get royalties totaling way more than just…"Five dollars!"

CHAPTER 27

Exhausted!

Sometimes, it would become extremely boring in the Ticket Office, and the phones would hardly ring at all, or maybe there weren't even that many envelopes to address or to stuff. As such, we Pages got to play games. Besides having to repeat the same sentences again and again with regards to ticket-availability, we constantly had to inform people of NBC's Burbank location and how to get there. The majority of the phone calls that we received stemmed from the Hollywood area. This was a challenging question for many Pages, most of whom were out-of-towners and/or out-of-staters. But for some of us, it was easy. For those of us who knew the city and the country, it was easier. For those who knew directions, it was easier still. For some of us who could fake it, it was just plain fun.

One day, a caller was seeking directions, and the Page who happened to answer the phone had not a clue as to how to guide the caller towards the Burbank facility. So this particular Page simply placed the party on hold, and said they would connect them with the Directions Department. Of course there was no real Directions Department. But I do believe I was the first one to take the ball and run with it, as I picked up the phone from my fellow Page, and said, "Directions! May I help you?"

The other innocent fun game we played in the Ticket Office was *Talk Show*. If the day was dead, and the phones again, were hardly ringing or whatnot, we all would play, *You're On With Herb!* At this time, I would press the flashing button linked to one of the multi-lines on the phone, and pretend to counsel a caller which, in a way, is really what we were doing with every caller that phoned in. We were fulfilling the emotional needs of those who just had to see Johnny Carson.

But probably one of the funniest things I ever heard (in a back-door kind of way), and that transpired in the Ticket Office, traveled out of the mouth of fellow Page, Roger Hyman, who was a wonderful guy to work with. Roger had a pleasant personality and pretty much made everyone feel at ease. One day he and I were working together in the Ticket Office. He answered the phone, and the person on the other end of the line, of course, wanted tickets to *The Tonight Show*. "I'm sorry," Roger explained, "those tickets are exhausted," meaning there were none available.

Before then, I thought only Pages could get tired. But now, apparently, so could tickets.

CHAPTER 28

Hangin' With Rear Lobby Joe

Besides the Ticket Office and the Ticket Booth, a few other thankless jobs that I had suffered as a Page involved working in the Research Department, and meeting and escorting game-show contestants to their particular place in the studio. Both assignments stationed me at the rear lobby of NBC, presided over by a young security guard/aspiring actor named Joe. It was part of Joe's job's to allow entrance and exit — via the security doors — employees, visitors and stars, all of whom had various reasons for making their way to the studio (much as when I was initially *buzzed-into* the studio on my first day of work).

Another part of Joe's job was answering the phone. Each and every time he did so, Joe would welcome the listener with the phrase, "Rear Lobby Joe." Hence, he came to be known amongst the Pages as Rear Lobby Joe.

That said, Rear Lobby Joe was a good guy, and a great conversationalist. He certainly helped me kill time on many occasions, such as when I was stationed near-by to rendezvous with various game show contestants or NBC Research individuals who were pulled from the street to test and pre-screen pilots and/or shows that had yet to air.

One interesting gentleman who signed-up with the Research Department happened to be the male nurse that was assigned to Rock Hudson as he lay dying of AIDS. I remember my ignorance in fearing that I would catch AIDS if I shook this man's hand upon greeting him. To his credit, he was determined to dispense any fear that I may have displayed. He set out to teach me a lesson that day — and he did. And wherever that male nurse is today, I thank him for it.

That said, on another day, and on a much happier note, I found myself once again shooting the breeze with Rear Lobby Joe. This time, NBC's back doorway introduced me to none other than Henry *The Fonz* Winkler of *Happy Day*s fame. Immediately, of course, I flashed-back to when I had met Winkler's *Happy* co-star, Ron Howard, approximately one-year before, at the feature film premiere of *Splash*.

Though an ABC show, and not associated with NBC, *Happy Days* was and remains one of my favorite TV classics. So, after meeting Howard and then Winkler, one dream after another proved to come true. Had they opened their eyes, it also could have been just as exciting for some game show contestants and researchers.

By this time in the Rear Lobby, I was accustomed to seeing celebrities. It had become a part of my job to retain a measure of decorum and dignity around popular TV actors and personalities, etc. On this particular day, my professionalism was in tact, as was my sense of irony.

As Mr. Winkler was standing there, signing the Rear Lobby Sheet stuck to the Rear Lobby Clipboard, right in front of me and Rear Lobby Joe, a few *Let's Make A Deal* game show contestants and research individuals were waiting to make their way inside the facility. One of the male *Deal* contestants was adorned in some form of pickle outfit. It was somehow decided that he would be the spokesperson for the others. "So tell me," he begins to ask Rear Lobby Joe, "do you ever see any TV stars come in and out of here?"

Time then stopped, as Rear Lobby Joe, myself and Mr. Winkler exchanged bemused looks. Time booted up again, as the silence of seconds was broken by Rear Lobby Joe, who replied to the man in a pickle, "Sure — I see TV stars all the time."

With that, Mr. Winkler smiled, and walked into the main building, right past the pickled- harried man, who remained oblivious as to which major television celebrity with which he had just missed a massive brush.

"Wow, that's cool," he continued.

"Yeah, it is," Rear Lobby Joe said with a subtle and somewhat snide reply.

Still, no matter how much Rear Lobby Joe tried to kill it, Mr. Pickle's enthusiasm would not die. "I think it would be great to see a TV star," he went on to relay, joyfully.

"It can be," Rear Lobby Joe responded, now with diligent deadpan.

Then, as if on cue, and this is no lie — in walks Andy Griffith, who would soon become one of NBC's biggest stars with the hit mystery legal drama, *Matlock*. It was like we were all playing some surreal edition of *Seven Degrees from Ron Howard*. Griffith was scheduled to meet network executives about *Return To Mayberry* — his TV-reunion-movie of *The Andy*

Griffith Show, which co-starred Howard, who also co-starred with Winkler on *Happy Days*.

As I stood there, silently in retro TV awe, Mr. Griffith signed his name to Rear Lobby Joe's studio roster, and the man in the pickle suit continued to jabber away with gleeful reiteration. "Geeze, what I would give to meet a TV star." And on and on and on he exclaimed.

Then, just as Mr. Winkler before him, Mr. Griffith looked up at me and Rear Lobby Joe, smiled, and walked into the main building.

CHAPTER 29

Vanna Speaks (with Brian Wilson)

I've talked so much about games and game shows associated with NBC, but I've so far neglected one of the most popular game shows to air on any network next to *The Price Is Right* on CBS. And that would be *Wheel of Fortune*, which was produced and created by talk show icon, media mogul and Donald Trump's main rival, Merv Griffin (who passed away in 2007).

In brief, the original host of *Wheel of Fortune* was Chuck Woolery, who would later host the multi-complicated behind-the-scenes *Scrabble* for NBC (and the syndicated *Love Connection*, which ignited the mean-spirited dating shows that followed). There was a period there when Woolery's *Wheel* went on hiatus, and then returned without Woolery, who was replaced by Pat Sajak and Vanna White (who had just released a memoir, entitled, *Vanna Speaks*).

Both Pat and Vanna, as they came to be known, were quite affable and amiable people. Vanna, in particular, was particularly down to earth and never once displayed any form of arrogance or a holier-than-thou attitude. In fact, she went out of her way to be nice to people, especially the Pages. From what I can remember, she made sure to recall the names of as many Pages as possible — including mine.

Meanwhile, back home in Rochester, my brother-in-law Sam, again newly-married to my sister Pam, had a mild-crush on Vanna, and was excited that I would periodically be assigned to work *Wheel of Fortune*. *Wheel*, like many of the game shows that taped at NBC Burbank, would have five episodes produced per day, three times a week — and therefore have many weeks of shows in the can in advance — ready for distribution. Both the daytime network and evening-syndicated versions of *Wheel* were taped at NBC, and that was a lot of shows. Johnny Carson's brother, Dick Carson, was then *Wheel's* main director, and it was always fun to see him walk around the set — as he looked very much like his famous brother. Unfortunately, however, I never got to meet Merv.

In any case, it was Vanna, out of the entire *Wheel* team, who stood out the most. As I said, my brother-in-law had a long distance thing for her and, because she was so approachable — and because she went out of her way to remember names (especially mine) — I asked her one day if she would sign a photo of herself for Sam on his birthday in 1984. Without the slightest hesitation, she agreed. "Absolutely," I remember her saying. "Not a problem." Consequently, she did indeed sign-over a photo, during a break from changing her famous wardrobe in between shots for *Wheel*. She ran to her dressing room, picked up one of her head shots, grabbed a black marker and autographed the photo to Sam.

People used to make fun of Vanna because she was paid hundreds of thousands of dollars just for turning letters on the *Wheel* board — a job that has allowed her millions of dollars in income ever since; a position that, due to ever-advancing technology of computers, is probably not even necessary today. In the old days, Vanna would actually turn letters. Today, all she has to do is press a button to switch the lights on of a particular letter chosen by a contestant. She doesn't even need to be there during the turning of the letters. The computers could handle it all. But what would *Wheel* be without Vanna? Who would Pat be? Just *Wheel* and Pat, that what's. And I can't think of a nicer woman in Hollywood who is more deserving of that job — which she has held for over twenty years — and success than Vanna.

Actually, some twenty years after I worked with Vanna on *Wheel*, I would see her at a local festival in Pacific Palisades, California. I attended the event with cousins, who were good friends with rock icon, Brian Wilson, the musical genius behind The Beach Boys — the group who introduced the world to the youthful dreams of California. Brian had accompanied my cousins to the festival as well, and it was he who noticed Vanna over to the distance, near the cotton candy booth.

At one point, Brian turned to me and said, "Hey, is that Vanna White from *Wheel of Fortune*?" I looked, and to my surprise, indeed it was. "Man," Brian said with such still-youthful excitement, "I am such a huge fan of hers." And I said, "Really? Well, I know Vanna. I used to work *Wheel of Fortune* as a Page for NBC. Would you like to meet her?"

"Really, man?!" Brian continued with enthusiasm. "You *know* her? I would love to meet her!"

That's all I needed to hear. As such, I walked over to Vanna, who again, I had not seen in over two decades, and said, "Hey, Vanna, I don't know if you remember me or not..." and before I could finish, she said, "Herbie! How are you?!" I was in shock. She was just as amiable and sweet as I had remembered her in 1984. In fact, it was she who became a bit nostalgic. "I've been doing the show for over twenty years!" she said. "Can you believe it?!"

"No," I replied. I could not. Then, after some more brief chatting, I mentioned that former Beach Boy Brian Wilson was a good friend of my cousins, that he was in attendance at the festival, and that he wanted to meet her. In a flash, she said, "Of course!" and we walked over to Brian and I introduced the two of them.

It's one of the coolest moments in my memory, NBC-related or otherwise. There I was introducing one of the legendary musical greats of all time to one of the most down-to-earth and sweetest famous California girls I had ever known.

Only in Hollywood could such things transpire.

Well, actually, Pacific Palisades.

CHAPTER 30

Harvey Levin Is Not Brandon Tartikoff

Today, everyone may know Harvey Levin as the ace-editor on the ever-increasingly popular pop-culture sensation known as TMZ.com. In the Big '80s, Harvey used to help out on shows like *Fight Back with David Horowitz* — a syndicated series that taped at NBC — and he would always roam the halls of the Burbank Studios.

The first time, I saw Levin, however, I did not recognize him as Harvey Levin. In fact, I thought he was someone much more important, like the president of NBC entertainment. It was all very innocent how it transpired:

I was walking down the hall with a Page supervisor. I see this dark-haired man in a non-Page three-piece suit walking toward us from the opposite way. I said to my supervisor, "Hey, look — it's Brandon Tartikoff. I just *have* to make a good impression," as I was only on the job for only a few weeks. So I walk right up to this dark-haired three-piece-suiter, and say, "Hello, Sir!" thinking it was Mr. Tartikoff. "I just want you to know that I am very excited to have recently been hired as a Page, and I will do anything and everything in my power to make you proud." Or some such nonsense.

So, then the man on the other hand of my shaking hand, just smiled politely and said, "Great to meet you" and walked away.

My Page Supervisor who was standing by me in shock and awe, simply asked what I was doing. I told him I was saying hello to Brandon Tartikoff.

"No," he said, "no you weren't. That was Harvey Levin."

We both just kind of laughed, as if stupefied at what had just transpired. As fate would have it, I did indeed finally meet Brandon some months later during my performance as one of *The Suppositories* (a fake musical group the Pages hurried to put together) at an NBC function in front of the NBC Gift Shop (of all places). Somehow, me and a few other Pages were recruited to sing some ridiculous song for an audience of the network's executives, including Tartikoff. After the song ended, Brandon, a brilliant television programmer (who succumbed to Hodgkin's disease in 1997 at the much too young age of 48), walked on over to me, placed his hand on my shoulder and said, "Good job."

I took that as a massive compliment coming from someone of his stature.

CHAPTER 31

I Helped Make A Wish Come True

Being a Page wasn't all laughs, and fun and game shows — for I had experienced many poignant moments on the job. For example, there was the one special night I had talked with the man known as Floyd, the famous individual who shined shoes for all the guests who appeared with Johnny Carson on his historic edition of *The Tonight Show*. Floyd's booth was located right outside Studio 1, where *Tonight* was taped. Floyd had a contract with the Guest Relations Department to keep all of Page footwear in tip-top shape. All each Page was asked too do, if they were any kind of a human being, was tip the man, a request with which I always made sure to fill.

I always enjoyed my visits with Floyd because *he* was the man with the stories. He met everyone and anyone with his decades-old position at the network. One tale in particular stands out: the one about the late Freddie Prinze, father to today's once-teen-heartthrob Freddie Prinze, Jr. (now married to Sarah Michelle Gellar, of *Buffy, the Vampire Slayer* fame, and who has just changed her name to Sarah Michelle Prinze, in honor of her spouse).

Freddie, Sr. was the star of NBC's huge hit, *Chico and The Man* (1974-78), which had taped in Studio 2, right across the hall from *The Tonight Show*. Tragically, at the height of his success on *Chico*, the elder Prinze committed suicide. A day or so before this horrible incident, Prinze had put a visit in to have his shoes shined by Floyd. As Floyd told me, "Freddie was feeling down — real down. He told me it was 'all falling apart,' and that things 'didn't make sense.' I didn't understand what he was talking about. He had everything going for him. Everything. But he just couldn't make it work. It was a real shame."

A real shame, indeed — and a message for a little Page with big dreams — the kind of dreams that Freddie Prinze probably dreamt...dreams that turned into a nightmare. I learned a lot that day from Floyd, and ultimately, from Freddie. I started to see things differently.

Consequently, and shortly thereafter, I experienced one of the greatest and most memorable moments of working as a Page. Periodically, we would be granted the opportunity to interact with the public in very special ways. Because I was considered one of the more sensitive Pages, I was many times assigned tours with disabled groups and/or those less fortunate.

One special tour, in particular, was given to a young group of visually-impaired kids from the Association of the Blind — and it became my favorite tour of all time. Those kids were so sweet. I would have to explain in every possible detail the tour to this special group who could hear but not see anything of what I was detailing. As such, I had to be more expressive than usual — as when we walked past the Wardrobe Department — where a regular tour group would never be allowed to stray, let alone touch any of the clothing or the mannequins. But with this group, the exception was made. "Come right up close to the mannequins," I said to the group. "Go ahead — feel the different material and textures."

Those beautiful kids were so excited to actually *feel* the costumes that were created; it was such a humbling experience. Every Page should have been as fortunate as I was to meet such special groups — to further appreciate the health we all take too much for granted. I was blessed that day by that special group; they offered me an insight that I otherwise would never had known.

Just like the day I conducted another special tour, this one a private tour with a very special little girl who I will call Mary. Mary was suffering from leukemia, and she was gifted the tour by the awesome *Make A Wish Foundation*, which grants special requests to special children. And Mary certainly was a special child. She was so sweet and adorable, and so happy to be on the tour, I was praying hard that I would have something unique to show her besides empty studios and the NBC national affiliates map that lit up towards the end of the tour.

Needless to say, it looked as though it was going to be a tough day. No major special or TV show was scheduled to tape that afternoon — not even a bad episode of *Scrabble*. But I carried on with as much energy as I could — and sure enough, miracle after miracle started to materialize.

As I was guiding Mary and her parents outside into the parking lot to at least attempt to showcase the interior of NBC's famous commissary (the regular tours would only have access to the exterior), my prayers gradually began to be answered.

First, Joan Collins, of ABC's huge-hit *Dynasty*, had somehow made her way onto the lot for a meeting of some sorts. "Look, Mary," I said swiftly to the adorable little girl beside me, "there's Joan Collins!" Mary's eyes lit up, brighter than that near-broken-down Affiliates Board. "Hey!" I continued, "How 'bout that? Pretty cool, right — seeing one of the biggest TV stars on the air right up close!?"

Mary's eyes gleamed again.

Then, not more than two minutes after we noticed Collins, Mary and I turned and there, walking right towards us was none other than Michael Gross — head of the fictional brood on NBC's then-super-hit *Family Ties* and one of the most popular TV dads of all time (a show, which also of course, featured my ol' pal Michael J. Fox).

I couldn't believe it. Mr. Gross was dressed in a formal tux, and I'm not sure why he was visiting the NBC lot that day, because (as mentioned earlier in this book), *Ties* taped at Paramount studios — in Hollywood. But it didn't matter why he was there; I was just glad he was — and Mary was ecstatic. But how would I get Mary to meet him?

Again, the angels were with me. Without saying a word, and from across the parking lot, I managed to get the actor's attention. I just peered into his eyes and somehow conveyed to him that I was conducting a very special tour with a very special little girl. In seconds, Mr. Gross walked on over to Mary, and I then went on explain to Mary and her parents what a super natural performer stood before us.

Mr. Gross picked up the ball. He immediately knew what was happening with Mary, and went on to spend five minutes with her talking about what it was like to be the dad on *Family Ties*. It was such an appropriate conversation about such an appropriate show, as Mary's dad was standing by, watching the conversation between his daughter and this big TV star. It was a beautiful moment — and there was no other way to say it.

I found out later that Mary died only a few weeks after our tour — and I felt so privileged to have received the opportunity to have been the liaison of even a few moments of happiness for her. In fact, meeting Mary made worthwhile my 18 months as a Page — and I mean that with all my heart.

CHAPTER 32

Tabitha, Marilyn and Susie Lynn

As I conveyed early on in this book, my job as an NBC Page saved my life in so many ways. After one of my first true loves dumped me like a hot potato in the humid Rochester summer of 1983 before I moved to Los Angeles, I felt burned to a crisp. I was an empty shell of a mortal; listless, directionless, and anything else *less* you can think of.

Then I became a Page. The basic six weeks training period (or boot camp, again as some have called it) allowed me to focus on other things besides the unrequited love of my life leaving me for some white trash, yellow-toothed fiend. (But again, I'm not bitter.) Now, as I began a new page in my life, I wouldn't have to think about her or him — especially when I met fellow Page Susie Lynn.

Susie Lynn was from one of the southern states, where her mom, who ultimately helped her get the job at NBC, was a noted television critic. Because of her mom's media connections, Susie Lynn was friends and/or associates with many TV stars and personalities, namely people like Lisa Hartman, then one of the mega-stars of the super hit CBS evening soap, *Knots Landing*. Susie Lynn's mom, Nora Lynn, and Lisa's mom, Hollywood publicist Jonni Hartman, were good friends. As a result, Susie Lynn and Lisa grew up together.

Keep in mind, too, that Lisa was also the star of the short-lived *Bewitched* spin-off and cult-favorite, entitled, *Tabith*a, which ABC aired in 1977. It wasn't the greatest show in the world, but rabid *Bewitched* fans like myself were spastic about it just being on the air — and keeping the original show's mythology alive (beyond the reruns of the original series). Yes, it's true that actress Erin Murphy, and her twin sister Diane — both of whom shared the role of Samantha's daughter on the original series, were not involved in any way with the *Tabitha* series. Many fans believed that ABC should have waited until at least one of the Murphy twins was old enough to play the character as a young adult (as Erin and Diane were merely in their mid-teens when the *Tabitha* series went into production). But that's not what happened. And for the moment, none of that really mattered. Susie Lynn knew Lisa Hartman, and in my pre-*Bewitched Book* author days, this was a very big deal. In many ways, it still is. The thing is, of course, I discovered by surprise that Susie Lynn was friends with Ms. Hartman. Here's what happened:

One night, Susie Lynn called me up and asked me if I would help her move. Apparently, she had many of her belongings stashed at Lisa's house, and she required some assistance relocating the items. Of course, I obliged, mostly because I was completely in love with Susie Lynn, and I would have done anything in the world for her. No two ways about it: the girl did it for me (even though she never actually did me — sad, but true). From the moment I met her, I forgot completely about my former Rochester love. Before meeting Susie Lynn, I didn't think it would be possible to put Sanya behind me, because not only had my heart been cracked in two, but it had also been hardened. But somehow, Susie Lynn melted it again, whether it was because of her southern bell twang, her big ol' hazel eyes, or her sweet physical form. Plain and simple: I loved her and, again, I would have done anything for her — including help her move (and we all know what a big deal that is in any kind of relationship; see the classic *Seinfeld* episode with guest star Keith Hernandez).

Needless to say, I arrived at the home of Susie Lynn's friend Lisa. I removed certain belongings, and delivered them to the premises of a woman named Marilyn, who was another friend to Susie Lynn's mom. Little did I know that both of these encounters would be my direct introduction to Hollywood celebritydom. Translation: I became personally associated with someone who was friends with a celebrity.

When I arrived at Lisa's home, Susie Lynn was there alone, and the elusive Lisa was nowhere to be seen. Now, again, remember — at this point, I had no idea that Susie Lynn's friend Lisa was the Lisa Hartman star of *Tabitha*. But I found out soon enough, once I started gazing around the premises — and noticed all the applicable photos. I think I actually said something really stupid — and I mean really stupid, like, "Geez, Susie Lynn — I didn't know that your friend Lisa was such a big fan of Lisa Hartman's?" It was like I was Lois Lane looking at Clark Kent and not knowing he was Superman without the glasses. But then Susie Lynn set me straight, ever so matter-of-factly. "Herbie," she said, point blank, "my friend Lisa *is* Lisa Hartman."

I freaked out. There was just no way I could control myself. "What?!" I screamed in near ecstasy. "Tabitha?! You know TABITHA?!!" Susie Lynn was extremely disappointed with my reaction, so much so, I was even embarrassed for her. "Herbie," she said condescendingly, "really!" Ironically, this sounded exactly like something Elizabeth Montgomery would say — on screen as Samantha — and off, as herself. Of course, too, this foreshadowed Susie Lynn's link to Elizabeth, which I'll get to later. But for the moment, I sounded like an idiot to Susie Lynn, and there was nothing I could do about it. I was in Lisa Hartman's apartment. I was in Tabitha's house. It was just unbelievably awesome. With each itemized move of Susie Lynn's stuff out of Lisa's house, I remained in awe. Susie Lynn just kept rolling her eyes back and forth, but again, I was helpless. Certainly, too, my fascination with Lisa Hartman didn't help my case in attempting to bed Susie Lynn; that train had long left the station — and it would never return.

Meanwhile, once we completed the move, Susie Lynn and I stuffed her belongings into her tiny Ford Escort and brought them over to Marilyn's house. Marilyn, again, a friend of Susie's Lynn mom (the TV critic from the south) lived in Beverly Hills in one of those mansions that appear to be carved into a mountain. You know? The ones that don't look like much from the outside, size-wise or by design, but once inside — damn. Very nice.

Marilyn seemed like a nice woman. She was a tiny sort, had a pleasant smile, and was very fond of Susie Lynn. Marilyn invited us in for a bite to eat after we completed the move, but Susie Lynn declined the offer. So we left. I took Susie Lynn home and the moving adventure had ended.

The next day in the Page lounge, Susie Lynn and I were reading the paper. I think she was looking at the Sports page, and I was reading the Entertainment section, still basking in the day-after-glow of being in Lisa Hartman's apartment the night before. I glanced at one particular showbiz column that I had been reading for years: Marilyn Beck's Hollywood update. As I was reading Ms. Beck's column, I turned to Susie Lynn and said, "You know something — I always wanted to meet her."

"Who?" Susie Lynn wondered.

"Marilyn Beck," I replied.

Now it was Susie Lynn's turn to be spastic. "What?!" she screamed on the Page sofa with her swift southern twang, "You met her laaaast nigggghhhhhtttt!"

"Uh?! Are you kidding me? That Marilyn is *this* Marilyn?" I squealed, as I pointed to and held up the paper. "Really?"

Then she said it again, "Yes, Herbie. *Really.*"

Once again, my face was reddened with pre-rosacea embarrassment in view of Susie Lynn's eyes. It would take me years to regain her respect — and how that transpired harkened back to *Bewitched*.

One day, after *The Bewitched Book* was published in 1992, Susie Lynn's media mom, the TV critic, interviewed Elizabeth Montgomery about one of her TV-movies, entitled, *Face To Face* (in which Elizabeth starred with her final love, Robert Foxworth). After the interview, Susie Lynn's mom put down her paper and pencil and said to Elizabeth, "You know, I just have to tell you — my daughter is very good friends with one of your biggest fans." Before Susie Lynn's mom could say another word, Elizabeth stopped her in her tracks, and spurted the name, "Herbie."

When Susie Lynn told me that story, I was elated. First, because my name was the initial thought that entered Elizabeth's mind when she was reminded of one of her biggest fans, and secondly because after Susie Lynn relayed the conversation, I replied with, "Really?!" "Yes, Herbie," Susie Lynn returned, this time, in kind — and with a great deal of respect, "Really."

CHAPTER 33

My Endless Dateline with NBC

Clearly, Susie Lynn was very special to me, so special that whenever another man gave her any attention, I became insanely jealous — like the night of the big Halloween bash of '85, which took place inside the NBC Burbank facility, between the KNBC and *Tonight Show* studios.

I'm not totally sure I recall everything that happened that night, but I do remember getting dressed up as Eddie Munster from *The Munsters*, and Susie Lynn ignoring me. I never consummated my relationship with Susie Lynn, and I don't think I ever even kissed her. It was definitely a case of unrequited love, but also one of a very strong friendship. We cared an awful lot about each other (and she later went on to marry a childhood friend of hers, though I think they're now divorced). But on the night of NBC's big Halloween party of 1985, we were estranged — and we became more estranged when everyone moseyed over to the KNBC hallway, where Susie Lynn started to dance up a storm with the resident male hunk news anchor, Jack Mustache. I was so pissed off and Susie Lynn embellished my anger. She just kept on dancing and dancing, and Jack just kept on trying to dance and trying to dance. *Dancing with the Stars*, it wasn't.

In the meantime, I'm all the way across the other hallway, in a drunken stupor, screaming, "You just keep dancing, Jack. That's right, just keep dancing. Susie Lynn may be yours tonight,"…and thankfully, someone then stopped me.

All I know is that Jack had the look of fear in his eyes and he was trembling. And I was satisfied with that. I later learned that, for months before, Jack had entertained Susie Lynn in his beautiful big ol', bad ass all-white,

$500,000 stucco condo in Long Beach. I, of course, just had my little studio apartment back in Santa Monica. That apartment was right behind the Taco Bell, at the corner of 17th and Santa Monica Blvd., and call me goofy, but I knew that somehow my place couldn't compare to Jack's place.

CHAPTER 34

The Victory Page Tour

One week, during my 18 month tenure as a Page, two new female Pages joined the troupes in a group, two or three classes behind mine. One was blonde, Molly, and the other was brunette, Lara, and both were truly awesome ladies, full of personality. Molly was sweet as pie, and Lara was the spitting image of a pre-*Friends* Courtney Cox, who had only recently been discovered in Bruce Springsteen's video for his breakthrough, mainstream hit, *Dancing in the Dark*. At the time, Courtney had been cast as one of the stars of NBC's *Misfits of Science* (a kind of *X-Men* with more than average mutant issues), and her star was on the rise.

Lara, meanwhile, was just a Page — like the rest of us and, like Molly, she was a giggly sort; immature, but in a very cute kind of way. I somehow ended up with Molly at the wedding of a mutual Page friend (who hooked up with one of the writers on *Days of Our Lives*). Molly and I didn't actually go to the wedding together, but we did spend most of our time together while at the reception. We were just friends, and maybe there were a few romantic sparks that night at the wedding party, but nothing that proved long-lasting. Also, too, Molly ultimately had a thing for one of the technical directors on *The Tonight Show*, with whom she ended up having a wedding party herself. So, things worked out.

Lara, on the other hand, was the one who truly caught my eye — and it wasn't because she closely resembled Courtney Cox, who besides her role on *Misfits of Science*, would also go on to play the periodic girlfriend/fiancé to my "good friend" Michael J. Fox on *Family Ties*. (Cox and Fox? There had to be something to that pairing.) So how did Lara and I hook up?

One day, a female Page named Patti Pen came into the Page lounge and said, "Hey — everyone — I've got a bunch of free tickets to The Jacksons

Victory Tour at Dodger Stadium? Anyone want a few?" Patti had access to the tickets because she was dating LA Dodgers Mike Marshall. I said I'd take two. I loved the Jacksons, and this was 1985 — one of the years that Michael Jackson was huger than huge. The Victory Tour was his way of helping his brothers, with whom he once performed as the original Jackson Five, to reap off his extremely rewarding and extensive career. I came to LA partly because I was inspired by the revolutionary charisma and dance moves of Michael's legendary videos for his super hits, *Billie Jean* and *Beat It*. Damn straight I wanted those Victory Tour tickets — and I could think of only one person that I wanted to accompany me to the concert: Susie Lynn. But it seemed that because I was so enthusiastic, I couldn't find her anywhere. It was like she had disappeared off the NBC lot.

Finally, however, I did indeed find her — in the ticket office. "Hey, Susie Lynn," I said.

"Yeah…?" she replied, deadpan, which was the usual response from anyone who had spent even a half-hour anywhere near the ticket office, or gosh-forbid, the Ticket Booth.

"Patti Pen gave me two tickets to the Jackson's Victory Tour," I continued. Let's go."

"I can't."

"Whadda'ya mean, you can't?"

"It's too expensive."

"You don't have to pay for them. I am."

"That's even worse. I know you don't have any money, and I can't allow you to pay for my ticket."

"What? Are you kidding me? This is the Jacksons! It's the biggest concert event of the year."

"No, Herbie. I'm sorry. I can't let you do it."

I was crushed. What's more, I couldn't help but think Susie Lynn was crushing me further, because of my crush on her — and that she was doing so out of spite. She knew how much that concert meant to me. She knew that it didn't matter how much the tickets were. I didn't care. I just very much wanted to go to that concert — and I wanted her to go with me. It would have been the ultimate date for us. But that's not how things turned out.

Rejected, I returned to the Page lounge with my three piece suit between my legs, head bowed and depressed. There, in the lounge, watching TV, was Lara. There was never any real attraction between us, but she sure was pretty. And she did have that Courtney Cox thing going on, so I figured, "Eh — why not?" So I asked her.

"Hey, Lara, you want to go to the Jacksons Victory Tour concert with me?"

"What about Susie Lynn?"

"Forget Susie Lynn. Do you wanna go?"

"Sure — I'll go."

So, a few nights later, there I was with Lara, Patti Pen and L.A. Dodger Mike Marshall at the concert. It was during the days when I just started to shave the unibrow between my eyes, and noticed that Mike Marshall had one, too. I thought to myself, "Man, why doesn't he shave his eyebrows. He looks horrible." That is to say, I know this was decades before the metrosexual world became acceptable, but still, the dude needed to work on his manscaping. Other than that, I don't think I said two words to him all night. All I remember him doing was grunting a lot with short replies to questions that either I, Lara or Patti asked him. If I was a Dodger fan, or maybe even a baseball fan, it probably would have meant something more to me to be on a double date with Mike Marshall. But all that mattered is that I was at that concert. Granted, I wish I had been there with Susie Lynn. But at least I was there, period — and the seats were great. We were up front — on the floor. And when Michael Jackson belted out *Billie Jean*, I went wild. I got on my chair, started doing those MJ moves, and Lara kept screaming, "You go, Herbie J. You go!"

Meanwhile, Patti laughed, and Mike Marshall, unibrow and all, just continued to grunt.

CHAPTER 35

Dimples

Yes, I have them. Dimples, that is. But for all intents and purposes of this book, the title of this particular chapter does not reference what may be considered attractive metamorphic facial features resulting from my toothy grin. Dimples is a reference to the name of one of the first karaoke bars in the country — and it was (and remains) located in Burbank, California, slightly up the street from NBC West on Alameda Avenue.

The rumors were rampant for weeks. Apparently, there was this local bar where anyone and their mother could go and sing, not lip-sync, but actually sing along with the music to any pop tune since pop tunes began. We all clamored for the spotlight at Dimples. And since partying was such a big part of being a Page, Dimples was the ultimate experience for us. So, of course, we'd party there every night. "Herbie, you going to Dimples tonight?" "We're going to Dimples, tonight. You wanna' go?" Everyone is gonna meet at Dimples later. You gonna be there?"

Absolutely I was gonna be there — whenever I had the chance. You kidding me? The Page who sang for *The Los Angeles Times* at *The New Let's Make A Deal*? You think he was ever going to miss out on an opportunity to sing for his compadres at the *Cheers*-like bar where everyone knew his name from his name tag?

My favorite songs to sing at Dimples used to be Michael Johnson's *Bluer Than Blue* and Lionel Richie's *Truly*. I especially embraced the opportunity to frequent Dimples because it was also another reason to hang out with Susie Lynn. She even tried a couple of times to teach me how to dance the two-step while some dude or dudette got up to sing a country song. I had come to like country music a great deal because of Susie Lynn. It was because of her that I became a fan of The Judds, Randy Travis and people like

Clint Black (who would later marry Lisa Hartman, which made everything so full-circle for me and Susie Lynn). Though I have to admit: Something strange did happen when I frequented Dimples. Not only did singing free up my inhibitions, but it also geared up my confidence — with other Pagettes, besides Susie Lynn, as well as other women, in general — specifically NBC TV stars. Like Courtney Cox.

One night at Dimples, and long before her super fame on *Friends*, and semi-regular role as girlfriend/fiancé to Michael J. Fox on *Family Ties*, Cox arrived in the club with her then-*Misfits of Science* co-stars, including Dean Martin's son Dean Paul Martin (formerly of *Dino, Desi and Billy* 1960's rock-stardom), Kevin Peter Hall and Mark Thomas Miller.

I thought this was kismet for sure. A few months before, I had a brush with Courtney, when she, along with the entire list of NBC stars, were promoting their new and old shows at the network's Fall Press Tour at the Century Plaza Hotel. At one glorious moment, and as fate would have it, Courtney happened to walk past me, smile and said hi in the hotel's lobby. I said hello back to her, and she gleamed, hoping for me conversation — and possibly a date. But like an idiot, I did not follow through.

Flashforward to this night at Dimples, and there she was again. By now, she was dating Dean Paul Martin who, unfortunately, died tragically in a small plane accident, during production of *The Misfits*. But he was there that night, as was Kevin Peter Hall, who played Harry in the movie and TV versions of *Harry and the Hendersons*, and who has now also passed away. But that evening in Dimples, there they all were — in front of me — in the crowd, as I was singing *Bluer than Blue* by Michael Johnson

I sounded pretty good that night, and Courtney seemed to enjoy it. It wasn't clear to me that she had remembered my face from the Century Plaza Hotel, and quite frankly, I didn't see how she could have. But I was at least going to attempt to have her remember me now. Mark Thomas Miller, however, wasn't having any of it — as he attempted to distract her by mocking me. But it wasn't working. I was singing too well and, as I said, Courtney was loving it. So, with my microphone in hand, I politely asked Mr. Miller to move from before my sight. He was stunned that I would make such a public and loud request, but in seconds — he was gone. Unfortunately, shortly thereafter, Courtney had left as well. Oh, sure she would later date Michael *I'm Batman* Keaton, and now, she's married to David Arquette. So… whatever. I hope she's happy and all that. But at least for a brief moment in Dimples time, she was mine.

Meanwhile, there was one other woman I had my eye on that night — a particular Pagette, who I will call Peggy. I had my eye on Peggy for a good portion of my contracted 18 months as a Page. But she was involved with someone else. Actually, she was engaged to a soap opera star that was way too many years her senior. I never really understood how a young woman of 25 would be interested in such an older man (50ish), until Tony Pete, of all people, clarified it for me by lifting his right hand, rubbing his two fingers together and implying that it was *all about the money*.

"Oh," I thought.

Anyway, after Courtney Cox left Dimples, Peggy was still there. Also in attendance was Susie Lynn, who had been ignoring me all night. And even though she could not figure out her feelings for me (friend or romantic love?), Susie Lynn probably wasn't too happy that I was attempting to seduce Courtney Cox. Again — no matter. I had downed a few drinks more than usual than night. I was ready for affection — and I was willing to find it from any available body — including Peggy.

I'm not exactly sure where I found the courage, but I somehow made my way over to Peggy. I literally grabbed her, brought her outside the bar, and started to kiss her — passionately.

"Herbie!" she screamed, though failing to stop me. "What are you doing?! What about Susie Lynn?!

"Forget Susie Lynn!" I said, just as I had told Lara with regards to the Jacksons Victory Tour. But this time, at least, I was *gettin' some*. That's right: Peggy could no longer fight what clearly became a mutual attraction, and she fell into my embrace.

"Oh, Herbie," Peggy pined. "I had no idea that you were such a good lover."

Well, we really didn't make love, right there out on the street. But we were swishing tongues pretty joyfully hard, so much so that I came to a better understanding of why they called that place, Dimples.

CHAPTER 36

Cheers

One night after work, a few Page pals and I decided to attend a taping of *Cheers*. By this time we had all actually worked the show — and any number of NBC sitcoms, game shows or specials, but the excitement of seeing a TV show tape in person was still there. And that was nice.

By the time we arrived at *Cheers*, actor Nicholas Colasanto, who played *Coach* the bartender, had succumbed to cancer. His replacement was Woody Harrelson, today a somewhat well-known former movie star (*White Men Can't Jump* leaps to mind) with a periodically-challenged personal life. At the time, Harrelson was only a few weeks on the job, and us Pages found it amusing that he appeared somewhat befuddled. Then very green in the business, Harrelson repeatedly and mistakenly referred to *Cheers* star Ted Danson as Mr. Danson, while in character throughout the taping. Woody should have been referring to Ted as Mr. Malone, who's fake first name was Sam. But I'm sure it didn't help matters that Harrelson's real first name and his character's first name were the same (Woody). Adding to this massive misnomer confusion was all the diva-doing being done on the set by Shelley Long, who would soon be leaving the show of her own accord (and be replaced by Kirstie *Star Trek II* Alley).

But the really fun part of the evening transpired when I was prompted by the show's warm-up man (the comedian hired to beef-up the audience energy) to sing my rendition of *Little Lovin'* by Neil Sedaka. *Lovin'* was a song that I would croon to the crowds of *The New Let's Make A Deal*, when I wasn't belting out *Always and Forever* (by Heatwave). I was performing during working hours on *Deal*. On *Cheers*, it was supposed to be my night off. But I wasn't complaining. You may have gathered by now, but I'm not one to be shy — and I enjoy attention.

So, I began to sing — gleefully. Meanwhile, on stage, behind me, there sat in his regular spot at the bar on the set was none other than *Cheers* actor George Wendt, who played Norm on the show. Wendt had clearly planned to relax and rehearse his lines in between filming. All of sudden, however, that all changed as he heard my wailing out the opening *Lovin'* lyric, "Mama raised me to be a man…!" Within minutes, I had the audience on their feet, clapping their hands and, well…*cheer-ing*. I looked behind at Wendt on stage, and he was dumbfounded. His jaw had dropped, and I was quite concerned as to whether or not he would be able to remember any of his lines that night.

Fortunately, he did — and the crowd loved him, mostly, of course, because I gave them a *Little Lovin'* lee-way.

CHAPTER 37

Mr. Excitement

No position or assignment as a Page compared to working *The Tonight Show starring Johnny Carson*. My personal experience with the King of Late Night TV was exciting, as were the moments I met those who were featured on his show, such as: Cyndi Lauper, Lucille Ball, Farrah Fawcett, John Travolta, Brook Shields, Paul McCartney (in a rare, rare outing), and Dionne Warwick and Raquel Welch (neither of whom were a bowl full of cherries). Welch, in particular, proved to be just a flat-out Jane-Seymour-esque pain in the ass. All she cared about was the lighting; how she was lit and how she looked when she was lit — which happened to be fantastic. In fact, she still looks great. I'm sure that's partly due to a few trips to the plastic surgeon (and clearly she went to the right one). But back in 1984, she was just being plain — as in plain difficult.

At the time, I had best remembered Welch from her legendary performance in the 1966 feature film, *One Million Years B.C.*, as well as in other motion pictures like *Fathom* (1967) and *Fantastic Voyage* (1966), and from her TV and general acting debut as a guest star on *Bewitched* (1964). None of these appearances, however, topped her performance this one night during rehearsal for *The Tonight Show*. Here, she just sat on that sofa and waited and waited for the lighting to be right, and barked and barked until it was, fuming at times, just like a spoiled little brat. I was hoping she would have at least partaken in a roll-around-*One-Million-Years-B.C.*-esque cat-fight with one of the female production assistants from *The Tonight Show* who was, along with everyone else on the crew, becoming quite frustrated with Rachel's anal antics.

Alas, that fight never transpired — and thank the Good Lord that additional *Tonight Show* guests, such as the aforementioned Cyndi Lauper and

Paul McCartney, proved to be a breath of fresh air — with nary an affected attitude in the bunch.

In fact, after Lauper's appearance and performance in particular, the Big '80s pop-music icon, best known for mega-hits like *Girls Just Want To Have Fun*, *Time After Time*, and the hauntingly-beautiful *True Colors*, treated fans in the hallway with such respect and cordiality it was astounding. She refused to reject not one individual waiting for her to sign her name in their autograph book or on their NBC Tour brochure. Further displaying her integrity, and after she completed conversing with what appeared to be the last fan standing, Lauper looked down a now empty backstage hallway, glanced over to me, who was watching all from aside, and asked, "That's it? There's no one else?"

I shook my head, shrugged my shoulders, gave one of those "Geez, no — I'm sorry" smiles, and said, "Guess not." "Oh, well," she intoned, turned and walked into her dressing room with a casual grace that I have yet to see again from any star, any place, at any time. She was utterly, utterly charming — and it was as simple as that.

The same may be said for Sir Paul McCartney, who was and remains a class act all the way. Just as with Lauper's performance on *Tonight*, there was a crowd of fans waiting for McCartney. He had just completed his gig on the show, which, I believe at the time, was a plug for his less-than critically-acclaimed or audience-embracing 1985 feature film, *Broad Street*, and its subsequent music soundtrack. But no matter. People still loved McCartney. I mean, come on, this was the #1 former Beatle. Mr. John Lennon's writing partner. The guy who wrote *Yesterday*, for Pete's sake.

When Cindy Lauper was signing autographs, there were maybe about 15 people waiting in line. When McCartney was around, the crowd of fans stretched into the widened main studio halls that were littered with game show prizes from *Wheel of Fortune* and *Sale of the Century*, and old props from *Sanford & Son*.

In any event, Paul was as sweet as could be with as many of those patient fans as possible. It was wonderful to observe. Whether you were male, female, straight, gay or Vulcan, everyone loved The Beatles. And there, before our eyes, was the legendary band's main man, the man with whom his four musical British brothers revolutionized pop sounds some twenty years before with their American debut on the air with CBS-TV's *The Ed Sullivan Show*.

In turn, during that Big '80s night on *Tonight*, Paul had an air about him, but not in a bad way. Backstage at the *Tonight Show*, after his performance, McCartney walked by his fans — a mix of various NBC employees and their families and guests, and wayward stragglers from the street who slipped passed security. Everyone's heart just seemed to skip a beat and, again, it didn't matter whether they were a man, woman or alien. McCartney left us all behind in his glorious charismatic wake, as each of our heads turned in unison to bid this Brit a friendly post-Beatle farewell. If NBC had ever given a *Magical Mystery Tour* version of its famous Studio Tour, this was it.

CHAPTER 38

My Photo Session With Brooke Shields

Beyond Raquel Welch, Cyndi Lauper and Paul McCartney, my most memorable encounters with *Tonight Show* guests remain to be Lucille Ball and Brooke Shields.

My contact with Shields transpired during her Michael Jackson days. At the time, many fans of both performers didn't know what to make of the Shields/Jackson romantic liaison. Some believed that she was hired as his beard or shield to cloak what everyone believed to be his true sexuality (that he was gay). Others believed that Brooke really had a thing for Mike. One industry insider told me that Shields sincerely cared for Jackson, so much so, that he felt constricted. As a result, he ended the relationship.

Me? I just wanted to meet the chick who starred in *The Blue Lagoon*. I merely had to figure out a way to do that — and it wasn't easy. Like many stars of the day (and today), Brooke walked around Hollywood with an entourage — lead by one individual. Brooke's leader happened to be her Mom, Terry, who was another breath of fresh air. At least, that's how I remembered it. Teri Shields called the shots. She ran Brooke's career. From what I could gather, she was doing a wonderful job. By the time Brooke was a tween, she was making millions modeling for top clients like Calvin Klein. She would later commence an acting career with motion pictures such as *Pretty Baby* and *Just You And Me, Kid* (with the late, great former NBC staple George Burns). But it wasn't until *The Blue Lagoon* that Brooke had established herself as a big-screen draw. Frankly, I wasn't too sure why she was on *The Tonight Show* when I met her, other than the fact that she may have been promoting one of her regular guest-spots on any number of the

Bob Hope specials this other great icon of the NBC family would produce and star in. This too, was years before the mild sitcom success she experienced with NBC and *Suddenly Susan*. So who knows? Again, all I knew at the time was that I wanted to meet her — and at least get a picture with her. "How cool would that be?" I asked myself. "To have a photo with the legendary model Brooke Shields? Would that be possible?"

Of course it would be possible. This was Hollywood. Anything's possible.

Fortunately, for me, as I approached Teri Shields, one of the Hollywood Angels (and I don't mean one of Charlie's), was literally on and by my side. A photographer for some teen magazine had been hired to cover Brooke's front and back stage appearance on *Tonight*. He seemed to enjoy my pursuit of a photo shoot with Brooke, and was only more than happy to oblige — especially when Mom Shields gave the okay. And she did. Again, Terry Shields wasn't the problem. It was her daughter Brooke. Once Brooke finished her chat with Johnny, she was whisked backstage to her dressing room, only to be stopped by her mom who had a request. "Uh? What?! Who?!" Brooke replied as her Mom whispered in her ear and pointed over to me.

"Oh, okay," Brooke finally said, as she and the teen-mag photographer prepped for a quick pic with me. Everyone was really cool with the whole thing — until of course I asked for a second photo. "Whatta' ya mean?" Brooke wondered.

"Well," I said, "you're just so tall. Lemme get a shot with me on me tippie-toes." She rolled her eyes and relented. "Okay, okay," she said, "but hurry up."

"Thanks, Brooke."

Whew! Flash 1 and Flash 2 were completed — and my photo shoot with Brooke Shields had ended. Brooke, Teri and the teen-mag photographer all then trailed away, with a promise that they would send me the photo. "Yeah, sure," I said to myself in disbelief. "That's going to happen." Yet, a few weeks later, to my happy surprise, the photo arrived. I looked good, if a little unshaven, with a shade of the hair stubbles on my face, and minus my Page jacket with only my vest on display.

But I was grateful for at least one thing: I had my wisdom teeth removed shortly before I had those photos taken with Brooke. As a result, brand new natural cheek bones became a prominent feature on my face. That was the ultimate model posture for the ultimate model encounter during the ultimate photo shoot with a model star.

I was just hoping that the photo of Brooke and me would have made it onto the cover of *Teen Beat*, or *Tiger Beat* or *16 Magazine*, or on and in whichever magazine that photographer worked for. "From there," I thought, "anything could happen." Maybe the photo would have been sold to *The National Enquirer*, *The Star*, or maybe even *The Globe* (that's an international magazine, right?). Maybe, as a result of it all, it would become clear to tabloid readers around the world that Herbie J Pilato was the real reason Brooke Shields left Michael Jackson.

CHAPTER 39

A Rivers Runs Through It

Joan Rivers, then on good standing with Johnny Carson (before she went behind his back to star in her own late night talk show for FOX, in one of the network's infant years), filled in for the King of Late Night TV on Monday nights. One such evening actress Bo Derek appeared with Rivers, and everyone involved will long remember the pairing.

Part of Joan's deal with NBC allowed her to pick and choose whomever she preferred and/or requested as a guest during her *Tonight* segments — and somehow, Derek was at the top of her list. At the time, Bo was best known for her role as the perfect looking woman in the 1979 film, *10*, as well as her status as the follow-up-wife to the late John Derek (behind Linda Evans and Ursula Andress).

By the end of Derek's appearance on *Tonight*, she was at the rock bottom of Joan's list of preferred guests — though one would never have thought things would have turned out that way from the onset.

Joan's introduction of Bo went well. Derek pranced on stage in a casual warm-up suit to thunderous applause. She was seated, and Joan was as nasty as usual, looking to confound her guest at every turn (which was the exact opposite of Johnny's winning technique). At first, Bo was grinding those perfect *10* teeth through most of the interview, attempting to refrain from expressing her true thoughts. But after a while, she could hold back no more. Out of the blue, Bo blurts out: "You know, Joan...I don't see any reason for you to put people down. You're an attractive, intelligent person. Why do you do it? Why are you so hurtful?"

No one could believe it. Joan could not believe it, nor could I or any one of my fellow Pages. If Johnny Carson himself was watching in his Malibu home, on his night off, we all were betting that even he could not believe it.

"Oh, you're sweet to say that," Joan replied through her now equal-to-Bo's-grinding teeth. But that was on-screen. Backstage was a different story. After the credits rolled and the studio emptied, Rivers screamed to anyone who listened, "I'm never gonna have that bitch on this show again. Who does she think she is talking to me like that? Embarrassing me on the air like that? That bitch! That bitch!! That bitch!!!"

Needless to say, Joan was just a wee-bit upset. Talk about being able to dish it out, but not take it? Man.

Some weeks later, at least, Joan calmed down a bit. On another Monday night when she hosted *Tonight*, John Travolta, of classic TV's *Welcome Back, Kotter* fame, was scheduled to be on her panel. By the time he appeared here with Joan, Travolta was also the star of two of the top-selling big-screen musicals of all time — *Saturday Night Fever* (1977) and *Grease* (1978), with a third harmonic flick, *Hairspray* (2007), now in the so-so status-file). Before he met with Joan on-screen, she decided to throw an on-screen surprise birthday party for another guest.

Lucky me — I was assigned the backstage position for Joan's show that night and was instructed to inform Travolta that his time with Rivers would be delayed. "Oh, great," I thought, "That's just great. Out of all the people in the world who come on this show, I have to tell John Travolta that he's required to wait a few minutes before he struts on stage with Joan Rivers."

I was one of Travolta's biggest fans. Like many Italian guys from the 1970s, I wanted to be Tony Manero (Travolta's role from *Fever*), Danny Zuko (*Grease*), and certainly beforehand, Vinnie Barbarino (his *Kotter* guise). I wondered, "Why can't I have been assigned to instruct some yodeling contest winner or a violinist that his or her appearance will be delayed?"

No such luck, that's why. So, I inhaled deeply and slowly walked towards Travolta's dressing room. As I was about three feet from the door, he rattled the knob from inside, exited, fixed his shirt collar and hair (of course), and headed for the green room (the place designated on all talk/variety shows where next guests wait to be introduced).

Meanwhile, there was no time for me to prepare any major discussion with him. I was forced to halt this superstar in mid-strut.

"Excuse me, uhm...Mr. Travolta?" ("Mr. *Travolta?!*")

"Yeah," he replied with his Barbarino/Elvis accent.

"Uhm...(gulp)...they won't...(gulp, gulp)...be needing you...(gulp, gulp, gulp,)...yet on the stage."

"Oh," he said, now sounding like a cross between Elvis and Andy Kaufman's Latka from *Taxi*, "Thank you very much."

"No," I should have said. "Thank *you* very much."

And thanks for nothing, Joan.

CHAPTER 40

Shadow Dancing

I was 23-years-old, working for a big TV network, living semi-large in the Big '80s, and I got to meet and talk with people like John Travolta. So, it really didn't get any better than that. Unless, of course, I also got to meet one of The Bee Gees, or at least their younger brother, Andy (who's biggest hit song was called *Shadow Dancing*, which may or may not have proved to be a metaphor for his relationship with his older brothers). Which is what happened during one of my other assignments in *The Tonight Show* hallway: I actually met Andy Gibb, little sibling to Maurice and Robin. Andy was working another show, in the studio across the hall from Johnny Carson's *Tonight* set. But I still managed to strategically place my Page chair to get a glimpse of the action on both of the shows that were taping that night in two different studios.

I had heard many things about the youngest brother Gibb (which, by the way, is how they came up with the Bee Gee moniker; it was the phonic sound of *B* and *G*, which stood for *Brothers* and *Gibb*). Two years before my stint with NBC, and meeting people like Andy, my life as a Page would be foreshowed by a former Page named Jeff Gordon, who I would encounter in an acting class at UCLA.

I had signed up for two classes: *Acting for Television* and *Directing for Television*, both of which were taught by famed director Don Richardson, who was one of the first to move from Broadway to the small screen during TV's *Golden Age*. Mr. Richardson would go on to direct historic episodes of NBC's *Bonanza* and then, later, *Lost in Space* for CBS. Mr. Richardson had also told me that he had instructed a very young Elizabeth Montgomery in one of her first acting classes when she was a teen in New York.

Strangely, there was now a link forming between Elizabeth Montgomery,

Andy Gibb, Jeff Gordon and NBC — all of which was threaded by two UCLA courses taught by Richardson. To begin with, on the very first day of acting class, Richardson asked his students who might be available to be his personal driver (as his eyesight was failing him and he could no longer drive). As he explained, the designated driver would be allowed to take the class for free. As I have always been someone who could easily be bought, I raised my hand in a flash, and got the job.

Consequently, Don and I became good friends. As such, I was privy to great behind-the-scenes stories of *Bonanza* (and how critical Don was of star Loren Green's acting), various Elizabeth Montgomery tales and more. But also, too, because of Don's class, I met an aspiring actress named Judy, and who had also known Elizabeth. But I would also befriend the aforementioned former NBC page Jeff Gordon, and a young actor who resembled not only Andy Gibb, but also *Xanadu* film co-star Michael Beck.

Of course, to complicate matters, Judy also had a great Andy Gibb story via Victoria Principle. At the time, I was pretty impressed with Judy because she knew all these celebrities — especially Elizabeth. But she came to know them only because she sold purses at some *foo-foo* shop in Beverly Hills. And apparently, Victoria Principle opened up to Judy about why she left Andy Gibb ("It just didn't work out"). Judy also observed Elizabeth purchasing a new purse, only to dump out the contents of her old handbag, and give it to a passer-by who had admired it.

It was all very serendipitous: meeting Don Richardson, who had taught Elizabeth, who bought a purse from Judy, who also met Victoria Principle who dated Andy Gibb, who now resembled a classmate of mine and Judy's at UCLA.

Anyway — so much for the convoluted back-story to what it was like to meet Andy Gibb. The bottom line is, when I finally did encounter the youngest Gibb brother, it transpired in the hallway between Studio 1, where they taped *The Tonight Show*, and Studio 2, where several music variety programs were completed, including the *Motown Summer Specials* featuring the talents of Smokey Robinson, Boy George and, at one point, Andy.

Because I was such a huge disco fan, meeting Andy was pretty much up there with meeting John Travolta — especially because Andy's older brother's wrote, performed on and produced the soundtrack for Travolta's super pop-culture big-screen movie hit of 1977, *Saturday Night Fever*.

But while meeting Travolta was a happy experience, encountering Andy was a sad one. He seemed like a lost soul, lonely and out of place. For my two cents, I don't think he ever got over his break-up with Victoria Principal. And I truly hope he's found peace in Heaven.

CHAPTER 41

I Stumped The Band (And Just About Everybody Else)

Shortly before my 18-month contract as a Page ended, Jesse Gomez (*I Remember Mama* and the mother/father of all Pages) took me to lunch. This was kinda'sorta' a monumental meal, as Jesse had been one of the many Guest Relations Personnel who had an "issue" with what they perceived as my cockiness. But since this was the Peacock Network, I really didn't think there was a problem. I figured, "Well, Brandon Tartikoff once thought my bud Michael J. Fox was too cocky, but then *Family Ties* became a massive hit because of the young actor's confidence. And at NBC as a Page, I was just being Herbie J."

At any rate, and according to Jesse, I had now proven myself as a solid member of the NBC Page team. And during our lunch (which, by the way, was outside at some park in Burbank), Jesse offered me an extension of 6 months to remain with the Page program.

I was honored, but declined. Not only did I want to start pursuing acting, full-time, but I also wanted to stick to my original contract. As I relayed to Jesse that day over a burger and fries, which were being invaded by mosquitoes and flies, "I signed up for 18 months as a Page, and that's where I'd like to end it."

Jesse was both disappointed and impressed. He very much wanted me to stay, but respected my decision, and thought leaving the way I did was a classy thing to do. As a result, we became friends that day. But had I stayed on as a Page, I may have indeed moved up in rank, possibly even becoming president of the network, or at least its programming division. Yet, alas, I had other fish to fry, and it was time for me to move on – though not before my TV appearance with Johnny Carson on *The Tonight Show*.

Beyond my limo runs with the stars, and my on-going relationship with *The Golden Girls*, the best part of being an NBC Page was playing *Stump The Band* with Carson, his right-hand man Ed McMahon, and musical maestro Doc Severinsen and his *Tonight Show* band.

Yep — that was every Page's dream. We all pined for it. To actually embrace the prize envelopes, while standing next to Carson, as he quizzed random audience members to name the tune that would…*stump the band?* That was heaven, or at least the closest any of us we're going to come to it on this Earth — and within the realm of our show-business understanding at the time.

I'll never forget when it was my turn to hold the envelopes. It was near the end of my 18-month run, and I had zero job prospects in sight. I was offered a six-month extension to stay as a Page. But I made a commitment for only 18 months — and I wanted to keep it that way. Meanwhile, too, various Page-loves had fallen by the wayside. Needless to say, I was depressed.

But then, just as with my darkest days in the time before I initially was hired as a Page, I received a call on another dark-turned-bright day. I was having lunch at the NBC commissary, when I was, uhm, *paged* into the Page supervisor's office, way over on the other side of the studio lot. The supervisor attempted to fool me into thinking I was in trouble (as I had so many times been before in their eyes — prior to my page profile in the *Los Angeles Times*). But I was not in trouble at all — and finally, the truth came out:

I was selected to be the Page for that night's round of *Stump the Band*. Apparently, it wasn't supposed to be me. A fellow Page was previously chosen, but now, due to bad behavior, was out of the loop — and I was in — with a makeup call and all.

It turned out to be a glorious night. As I was standing there next to Carson, holding those envelopes, seeing the craziest people attempting to stump the band with the most ridiculous songs (*The Bus People?!*), it felt like I was having some kind of spiritual experience. In many ways, of course, I was experiencing just that. While Carson was joking with McMahon and Severinsen, and one man in the audience was thinking out loud with his tongue pushed all the way to one side of his cheek, it was as if my previous 18 months as a Page were passing by me in a flash — as if I was traveling towards the *light in a tunnel.*

I later found out that I received more *Stump the Band* airtime than any Page in history. Because of my slight height, while standing next to Johnny I managed to get my mug in almost every frame (which allowed my parents at home in Rochester — in a pre-VCR age — to take pictures of me from right off the TV set). Pages in the past were lucky to get their knees on camera, but I got to display my entire pin-stripped, name-tagged bod — from head to toe. So much so that *Tonight Show* director Bobby Quinn (who passed away in 1999) became quite aggravated, and wondered, "But who the hell is this kid? He's in every frame!"

Had Mr. Quinn asked me directly, I would have invited him to read my nametag, and said, "My name is Herbie J, with no period. And you just helped me write the final chapter in the book of my life as a Page for NBC.

Afterword

I had more fun writing this book than any previous publication. After telling these NBC stories for years (at parties, at pools, at pool parties, in daily conversation, etc.), I finally put the pen to yes — the page (if I may use that metaphor one last time). So, I would like to thank all the NBC stars, executives, and Guest Relations Representatives with whom I had the privilege to work, especially: Harry Anderson, Conrad Bain, Michael J. Fox, Gary David Goldberg, Sandra Santiago, James B. Sikking, Eba Hawkins, Jesse Gomez, Mary Maggio, and former Pages Marypat Flynn, Jesse Gomez, Jeff Gordon, John Holmes, Kris Keller, Steve Leon, Jeff Meschel, Marty McClintock, Mike Nananni, Karen Powers, Horris Smith, Tina Stewart, and so many others whose names have conveniently escaped me (or at least been conveniently replaced by fake monikers in this book). In either case, you all know who you are.

I would also like to thank the entire family of professionals at BearManor Media, including publisher Ben Ohmart — who's continued literary loyalty and respect for all media things classic is truly an inspiration, his wife and executive assistant Mayumi Ohmart, and succinct typesetter Brian Pearce. I would also very much like to acknowledge author Charles Tranberg (*I Love The Illusion: The Life And Career of Agnes Moorehead* and *Fred MacMurray: A Biography*), who introduced me to BearManor Media (the publisher of Chuck's brilliant books). May special gratitude also find its way to: Gretchen Harris Keskeys, who wrote such a sweet foreword (to a sometimes biting-book), graphic designer Matt Hankinson, who once more created an eclectic cover for one of my tomes, and my right-hand editor Jaclyn Garfinkel, who organized my memory and words with superior efficiency and grace.

I would also like to thank photographers Joe Vitti (for the photo of myself that appears on the front cover and on page 70 in the Photo Gallery) and Salvatore Amato (for the photo of me on the back cover). The additional photos and illustrations that appear inside this book, or on its front and back covers, are from my personal collection.

All that said, there are so many other wonderful stories to tell.

For example, there was the time that *Night Court* actor Richard Moll picked me right up over his head at an NBC Press Tour. Another time, I met George Clooney, son of KNBC news anchor Nick Clooney (brother to songstress Rosemary Clooney). Young George, then featured on NBC's *The Facts of Life*, once passed me in the NBC halls, and he looked at me with eyes to seemed to say, "So, who do you think you are?" A similar moment later transpired with John *ER/Full House* Stamos, then working on the short-lived and poorly-done NBC comedy, *You Again!* (which co-starred Jack *The Odd Couple* Klugman). Then, of course, there were the weekly jaunts up to the accounting office to meet with a cute little hottie who had more of a fantasy thing for Sylvester Stallone then caring to have any kind of reality thing with me.

Then, of course, too, there was the time I visited the office of Joel Thurm, then President of NBC Casting. Though Mr. Thurm was always polite and respectful towards me, his secretary was quite the opposite (which is usually the case in these type of Hollywood scenarios). Apparently, she had an issue with me leaving a massive photo of myself on Mr. Thurm's desk, with the hopes that I would be cast as the star of a pilot for a detective series featuring a short private eye called *Half-Nelson* (the lead for which ultimately went to Joe Pesci).

We would also, of course, find out more about the name of Herbie J Pilato, detailing how my awesome Pagette pal Tina Stewart (who did a rockin' impersonation of Tina Turner singing *What's Love Got To Do With It?)* used to refer to me as *Mr. Pilto* — or how the equally great (and witty?) Pagette Jennifer Hosack, who upon our first meeting, referred to me as *Herpes*.

Clearly, there's just so much more to tell (all) and, either way, I guess we're just gonna' have to wait and see what the response will be to this book. If it's not so great, I'll move to Australia, or maybe just stay here in America and sell ties at Sears. If this book is a success, I will have absolutely no issue with writing the sequel, *NBC & ME, TOO: More Pages Of My Life As A Page In A Book.*

About the Author

Herbie J Pilato is a writer, actor, TV producer and director, and singer/songwriter who was born and raised in Rochester, New York (on Erie Street across from where now stands Frontier Field). He attended various parochial elementary schools in the Rochester area, including: St. Peter and Paul's, St. Augustine's and St. Anthony of Padua. He graduated high school from the esteemed Aquinas Institute, attained a B.A. in *Theatre Arts* from Nazareth College of Rochester, studied TV & Film at UCLA, and served his Internship in Public Relations at NBC Television in Burbank, California. Today, he is the author of several television literary companion books, including *The Bionic Book* and *Life Story — The Book Of Life Goes On* (both of which were published by BearManor Media in 2007), *Bewitched Forever* (Tapestry, 2005), *The Bewitched Book* (Dell, 1992) *The Kung Fu Book of Wisdom* (Tuttle, 1995) and *The Kung Fu Book of Caine* (Tuttle, 1993). Herbie J has also served as an editor for various websites (such as TV-Now.com, UPNTV.com, PAX-TV.com and MediaVillage.com), contributed to many magazines (like *Starlog, Sci-Fi Entertainment, Retro Vision, Classic TV* and *Remember*), and has made hundreds of radio and TV show appearances (including *The E! True Hollywood Story*, A&E's *Biography*, and *Entertainment Tonight*). As an actor, Herbie J has performed on TV soaps such as *General Hospital* and *The Bold and the Beautiful*. Some of the TV programs he has produced, include Bravo's hit five-part series, *The 100 Greatest TV Characters* and TLC's *Behind the Fame* specials. He's also served as a consultant on Nora Ephron's *Bewitched* feature film and on the first-season TV-DVD releases of *Bewitched, Kung Fu* and *CHiPs*.

Herbie J recently toured with Nik & the Nice Guys ("America's #1 Party Band") as *Frankie Valli* in the group's *Rock Icon Tribute Artist Show*, and released his first music CD (entitled, *Two*) in 2007. He is presently developing several new television shows and feature films, while his future books for BearManor Media include: *Twitch Upon A Star: The Elizabeth Montgomery Story*, *Kung Fu And The First Journeys of Caine* (a revised and combined edition of his previous two *Kung Fu* books), and *Trek's Saturday Morning Star: The Colorful Companion To The Animated Edition Of The Original Star Trek TV Series*.

NBC & ME: MY LIFE AS A PAGE IN A BOOK 163

NBC & ME & JOHNNY: This photo of me playing *Stump the Band* with Johnny Carson on his *Tonight Show* was snapped by my Dad (a.k.a. *St. Pompeii)* right off the TV set back in Rochester in 1985, ten years before he passed away. At the time, he and my Mom *(St. Frances)* were still living in the beautiful townhome at Greenleaf Meadows (to where we all moved from our awesome red brick house on Erie Street).

www.ingramcontent.com/pod-product-compliance
Lightning Source LLC
Chambersburg PA
CBHW051108160426
43193CB00010B/1364